the will of god
in other words

LIST OF AUTHOR'S PUBLISHED WORKS

Nihil Obstat: RALPH RUSSELL, O.S.B., *Censor Deputatus*
Imprimatur: B. C. BUTLER, *Abb. Praes.*

8 September 1962

the will of god in other words

A PRESENTATION FOR BEGINNERS

by

Dom Hubert van Zeller

TEMPLEGATE
SPRINGFIELD, ILLINOIS

To Mary Vander Vennet
in the hope that she may come upon it one day

Contents

☿

How It Works   1

THERE can hardly be a better practice in the
spiritual life than that of meeting everything as an expression of the will of God. Phrases
like 'if God wills' and 'it must be the will of God'
and 'may God's will go with you' come naturally
to the devout. People in certain traditions of
Christian life say these things all day long and
mean them. God's will becomes for them the
standard of everyday decisions and the background against which life happens. Nothing
furthers the supernatural point of view so effectively as the cultivation of such a habit. It can
be seen as an extension of the *Our Father*, as an
identification with the disposition of Christ, as the
application of 'I came not to do my own will but
the will of my Father who is in heaven' to our own
human concerns. It can be made to sum up the
whole of our Christian service. But 'God's will'
is not just a magic formula, a password which
opens all the gates, a label to be stuck on to
luggage which need not be thought about for the
rest of the journey. God's will, in other words, is
not a superstition.

God's will. It can mean so much—and so
little. We accept as God's will the outbreak of a

revolution, the breaking of a dam which means the destruction of homes and harvests and lives, the loss of a leader or of someone we have loved personally. We accept also as God's will a tiresome interruption, the missing of a train, an obstinate tap, an alarm which fails to go off. There is nothing wrong in accepting such circumstances as manifestations of God's will— indeed we should train ourselves to do so—but we must be careful to avoid the misconceptions which would rob the exercise of its value. Even granted that we really mean what we say when we hail an event as God's will, it is important that we should mean what is right.

In the first place it is a mistake to imagine that the disastrous is the most fitting occasion for the doctrine's application. The implication would be that God is forever planning horrors for mankind and that by recognising them as coming from him we can at least prevent them from being any worse. It pays God no compliment to assume that he is responsible for everything unpleasant which happens to us. Much of the unpleasantness which we suffer is entirely our own fault, and allowing that much of it may come from the malice and stupidity of others, we do wrong to put all the blame on God. Later in this study we shall see how God *permits* evil while he *wills* good. We should guard against concentrating on what he permits to the exclusion of what he wills.

While it may be easier to see the will of God in what is painful than in what is pleasureable it is nevertheless true that God designs us more for happiness than for sadness. Sadness is a negation of happiness: it is not something which exists in its own right. Sadness may be very necessary to us, and in this sense it can be looked upon as a good, but it is not something to be aspired to and enjoyed as a positive possession. So it is strange that we should connect it with the will of God more often than we connect happiness with the will of God. 'I suppose I have to accept this trial as God's will,' we say with a sigh. Do we so readily shout with joyous recognition of God's will when something happens which pleases us? Gratitude gets just as near to the will of God as resignation.

It is important then to think of God's will as something positive, as a vital force with which we can become identified, and not merely as something restrictive and imposed in virtue of God's prerogative. In our recognition of God's will it would be something of a waste to stop short at bowing to the inevitable. God's will should be an invitation, a challenge to the service of love. Once we grasp the truth that God wills man's happiness we ought to be able to hail joy as the gift of God, as an incentive to recollection, as among the clearest indications of divine providence.

Another trap which lies open in the estimation of how God's will touches our affairs is the view we grow up with of God himself. If we are honest with ourselves do we not regard him as

9

one who manoeuvres us into positions which suit his plan and from which we cannot escape except by his miraculous intervention? The misconception arises partly from the false idea of prayer which we learn as children, partly from the idiom of piety which looks more to the extraordinary than to the ordinary ways of grace, and partly from our quite understandable tendency to judge the mind of God by what we know of our own.

First, what are we told about prayer? We are given to understand that it will get us out of every difficulty. From our earliest infancy the belief is drummed into us that if we repeat our petitions often enough we shall get what we want. Faith and perseverance: armed with these two we cannot miss. Now all this is perfectly true, but not in the sense that we normally understand it. Prayer *does* get us out of every difficulty—by so building up our inner reserves that we meet every difficulty and rise above it. If we repeat our petitions often enough we *do* get what we want— because we come to want God's will even more than we want an answer to the particular petition we are making. Given faith and perseverance we cannot miss—since in proportion as these qualities deepen we get closer to our true goal, which is God.

Sometimes, it is true, the more obvious meaning of the doctrine is verified. We pray, and the obstacle vanishes. We place complete confidence in the power of God to work a miracle, and the miracle (to everyone's surprise including our own) happens. We make up our minds never to give up asking, come what may, and after a while we are rewarded with exactly what we have asked for. Instances of this sort are happily common: they strengthen our belief in the power of prayer and provide occasions for showing gratitude to God. The thing to remember is that such examples of cause and effect are not the only ones which prove the value of prayer, and that those which show it less clearly are evidence of greater faith, greater love, greater trust and generosity.

The next source of misunderstanding is the peculiar phraseology of popular devotion. Printed prayers, hymns, exhortations from the pulpit, little ferverinos which we read in letters from religious men and women: all seem to suggest that the ways of God belong to a quite different world from the one we know, and that if we are to tap the sources of the spirit we must use a formula which we would never dream of using in our dealings with people. It is true of course that the order of grace does not operate according to the laws of nature, but at the same time there must be an affinity between the two or we would never begin to understand the order of grace at all.

Speaking about the way in which grace works, our Lord uses the illustration of seed growing to maturity in the field. The farmer sows, goes home and attends to other things, comes back at the proper time, sees how the development has been getting on, and eventually reaps. The implication here is that the dealings of God with man follow a more or less accepted course, and that only on special occasions do they deviate into the extraordinary. Yet if we went by the idiom of piety we would be assuming a different manifestation altogether. We would look for God's will in the spectacular, await God's mercy in the dramatic, expect God's peace to reveal itself in placid contentment.

The trouble is that we have our own ideas about how God's will is to be revealed, and since these ideas are coloured by self-interest they are almost always wrong. Like Naaman the Syrian we instinctively leap to the grandiose, picturing to ourselves a sensational cure of our particular leprosy, when in fact God operates in a commonplace setting and through materials without glamour. The error is a not unusual one: James and John fell into it and were corrected by our Lord who called them 'sons of thunder'. If we turned more often to the gospel for our cue as to how God's will operates we would get nearer to the truth than by studying the candy-coated opinions of the devout.

A missioner prays for the grace of martyrdom. Fine. Ideally speaking, and all things being equal, there is nothing much higher that he could pray for. But what if it is emotionally and not ideally speaking? What if all things are not equal? And in fact they never are. Grace infallibly comes in answer to the missioner's prayer but it is not the grace expected. Perhaps he is sent home to the mother house to do the accounts or answer the door. Not at all the martyrdom he wanted, not at all the heroism he pictured to himself. But a grace nevertheless, and the will of God nevertheless.

Or take a less obvious example illustrating the same theme. A wife prays that her alcoholic husband be released from his slavery to drink. Nothing can possibly be wrong with that. For the husband drink is an evil, and she is praying that he be no longer tempted. Grace, again, infallibly comes. But not necessarily in the form of a physical cure. The man does not suddenly find himself disgusted at the sight of a bottle. The smell of liquor does not put him off his food. What happens is that something happens inside his character: he is given a chance of seeing more clearly and acting more resolutely. He is perfectly free to act upon or reject the grace. The attraction to drink may remain as powerful as ever but there is an added strength with which to meet it. Now say this man fails, and goes on drinking with undiminished purpose, is the wife to assume that her prayer has been fruitless? Not at all. What she should do in this case is to see that no obstacles are put in the way of the ordinary course of her husband's cure. If she is driving the man to drink by nagging at him, she is counting too much on a miracle when she prays that he may give it up. It cannot be too much insisted that the grace of God, which is the same as the will of God, comes to us normally through normal channels. Grace builds upon nature; it does not jump over it unless for some reason God wills a miracle. The best preparation for supernatural intervention is the right use of the natural. Where ordinary means are provided, ordinary means should be employed. It is when ordinary means are not provided that we can start thinking about miracles. It is comforting to reflect that whether ordinary or extraordinary, all means directed by a right intention towards good come under the providence of God. God's will does not have to wait for the heavens to part before it declares itself.

Now for the third of our mistaken approaches to the subject—the tendency to read God's mind by comparison with our own. Experience of our mental processes shows us a directing organ which is highly variable. We change our minds every few minutes, we come under the influence of other minds, we are never absolutely sure what our mind on any given subject really is, we make up our minds on the spur of the moment to meet a particular situation, there are subjects about which we genuinely believe ourselves to have a completely open mind, and there are whole areas of life in relation to which we have no mind at all. (How often in the day do we say 'it doesn't interest me' and 'I don't mind'?) God's mind does not work in this way.

God does not change. He is eternally the same. If God could change his mind he would stop being God. God is never swayed by our prayers as we are swayed by the pleadings of fellow human beings. Yet we talk as though the intensity of our faith were able to influence the mind of God. Our prayers cannot be stronger than God's decisions or God would have to abdicate in favour of his creatures. It is perhaps here, in this matter of the otherness of God's mind from ours, that the source of all our confusion lies. If we could grasp what is meant by the everlasting sameness of God, we would get a better idea of how his will operates in the world and in our own souls. We would understand how his mercy is always waiting for the sinner to repent, how his presence is always with us, how his love is the only reason why there is any love in us at all, how impossible it would be to misplace whatever trust we put in him.

Not only can God's mind never change but his love cannot change either. We human beings possess a different kind of heart. Our hearts are as variable as our minds. But with God his love is the same as his will—eternal and unchanging. Human beings love now one person, now another. Sometimes they love God, and then another love comes along and the love of God dies down. It is one of our sad human limitations that there is room in the heart for only a certain amount of love: love in this life is incomplete: we are physi- cally and emotionally incapable of loving everybody indiscriminately all the time. But with God this is not the case. God does not change towards people as they change towards him and towards one another. With him there is no division or sequence of operation as regards love. And because his love and his will are one, his infinite and universal love must mean an infinite and universal will towards the good of man.

The implications of this touch us at every point in our lives, at every waking and sleeping moment. It means that loving us as he does, and in virtue of his infinite wisdom knowing exactly what is best for us, God never stops willing our highest happiness. In all that we do God wants us to aspire to the perfect happiness which is his alone to give. Our Lord tells us to ask 'that our joy may be full'. It is important that we appreciate the attitude of God towards his creatures, establishing firmly in our minds that his love and his will are one, because very often we follow our Lord's injunction to ask and are rewarded with no sort of joy at all. If God is forever willing our highest happiness, how is it we taste so little of it? If God is almighty, can he not bring about our happiness more often—especially when we ask him in his Son's name to do so?

The answer to such misgivings is seen at once if again we compare God's way of loving with our way of loving, God's way of willing with our way of willing. In our case there are division, opposition, starting and finishing. In God's case everything is one, and there is no beginning or ending. Take first our human way of acting where love and making decisions are involved, and then see how God's way is bound to be different. Say you have a mother who loves, devotedly but injudiciously, her son. The love may be lasting and self-sacrificing, but because it is human it will be vulnerable. The son pleads and the mother gives in. The mother may know in her heart that it is a mistake to give in, but her love is in opposition to her judgment. So in consenting to her son's demand she is willing for him the lesser good. In the case of God's love for us the situation is quite different. His will cannot oppose his love because they are the same thing. He cannot 'give in' to a mistaken course of action on the grounds that love excuses everything. Yet is not this what we imagine him to be doing all the time, what we hope he will do next time we pray for something which we want very much?

When we speak of God 'consenting' to our request, we should not think of an alteration taking place in the mind of God. It is not as though he had decided in the beginning upon a course of action in our regard, and then, because of the new light shed upon the matter by us in our prayer, is now prepared to fall in with our idea. All along he has willed what was most for our good: the only thing our prayer has done is to bring this will into play. Moreover this prayer of ours which has seemed to have had such telling effect was not an invention of our own: it was inspired by him in the first place or we could never have made it. On the occasions when our prayers are heard in the terms requested what has happened is simply this: God, willing a certain effect to result upon the condition of our praying for it, has given us the light to see what was wanted and the grace to ask for it.

In view of what has just been said it should not be difficult to understand how prayer is essentially a rising of the soul to meet the will of God. If we think of it as a drawing of God's will down from heaven so that it coincides with ours we think of it mistakenly. Even the specific act of petition, so often insisted upon in the gospel, is to be valued not for what it manages to get out of God but for what it gets out of us. It cannot get out of God what God has not from all eternity wanted to give.

If we look again at the two illustrations given earlier we can follow, now that the idea has been developed further, a wider application of the same principle. Thus had the missioner and would-be martyr been granted his opportunity of laying down his life for Christ he might not have made as good a job of it as in the providence of God he was granted to make of his book-keeping and answering the door. The merit attaching to any work is measured solely by its conformity to the will of God. God rewards only his own works, the works occasioned by his own will. Nobody understood this more clearly than right motive for doing so it was no use delivering one's body to be burned. Without charity, St. Paul claimed, martyrdom was vain. And what is charity but the union of man's will with the will of God? Love in this context is not the emotion but the conformity. If we unite our human will with the will of God we have charity, and we can do that whether we are called to the degree of charity which is crowned by martyrdom or to the less exciting degree which expresses itself in the commonplace. The one qualifying factor is the will of God.

The second illustration is more complex but the providential exercise of grace can be traced in the same way. The woman prays for her husband, and so far as outward results go the prayer is fruitless. But who is she to judge? For all she knows there may be a dozen good reasons, seen only by God, why her husband should be allowed to fail. His present weakness may prove the impulse to a penitence of heart which he never would have arrived at had he jogged along in a state of self-satisfied temperance. Without his repeated lapses she herself might never have turned to God for help. Her trial of faith and hope, combined with his humiliation, may be giving great glory to God. Others, unknown to this struggling couple, may be receiving grace as the result of the suffering. God has a wider screen presented to him than man has, and it is a mistake for us to question the often bewildering permissions of his will.

To conclude this section, and by way of commentary, it is worth quoting from a document found on the body of an unidentified Confederate soldier during the Civil War. 'I asked God for strength that I might achieve; I was left weak that I might learn humbly to obey. I asked for power that I might lead, and win the praise of men; I was given weakness that I might feel the need for God. I asked for health that I might do greater things; I was given infirmity that I might do better things…I got nothing that I asked for, but everything that I hoped for. Almost despite myself my unspoken prayers were answered. I am among all men most richly blessed.' Whether or not he was a Catholic, whether or not he had any theology, the writer of those lines had learned what was meant by the phrase 'the will of God'. There is always an inwardness to the way in which God treats his creatures, and we are given the grace of faith precisely for the purpose of accepting that inwardness and acting upon it. There is an outward way by which our lives are conducted but it does not carry us far enough. The external may be, indeed most often is, misleading. So with St. Paul 'we look not at the things which are seen but at the things which are not seen; for the things which are seen are temporal, but the things which are not seen are eternal.' The will of God is in the things which are seen (or they would not even come to light in the first place) but to see it there is only half the battle. The easier half. The difficult part is seeing the will of God in the obscure, the frustrating, the apparently inconsistent and even contradictory. Difficult but not impossible: we are given the grace to trust.

What Follows From This 2

O NE of the main conclusions to be drawn from
what has been said so far is that God's will
shows itself not as a ruling which comes from
without, superimposed upon life as a religious
extra, but rather as a force in life and through
life. It is something the effects of which we see
outwardly and acknowledge, but the reality of
which is an abiding part of life itself. Indeed it *is*
life itself, because without God's will life would
not only be meaningless but would be non-
existent. 'The wind cannot be seen,' said Soc-
rates, 'but can be known by what it does,' and
just as the waves on the sea and the leaves on
the tree bear witness to the activity of the un-
seen wind so the circumstances of our lives and
the events of history bear witness to the unceas-
ing and underlying operation of God's will.

So if we are looking for God's will, and we
come into this world for nothing else but to
search out his will and fulfill it, we know where
it is to be found. It is everywhere around us
in the happenings of life, it is inside us drawing
our souls towards co-operation and union. Admittedly we may often find ourselves completely
in the dark as to which of two or more courses to

follow is the one God wills us to choose, but this does not mean that God's will is not there for us to discover. God does not suspend his will, as if he were lifting the map out of our hands and telling us to get on with our journey unaccompanied by his grace, because if he did we would cease to be. It is his will that 'conserves' not only us human beings but the whole of creation. The universe (the cosmos and space and all the rest of it) hangs upon the will of God, hinges upon the will of God, proceeds in its pace and rhythm according to the will of God.

When all this has been said it can be seen how some ideas are really too big for human language and that the will of God is one of them. To claim that creation 'hangs' upon the will of God, 'hinges' upon the will of God, is to suggest no more than that God supports the work of his hands as a pear-tree supports its fruit and that he keeps the earth spinning round as the mechanism in a fairground keeps the painted wooden horses in musical circulation. But what the will of God does is far more than this. It gives being itself. Take away the will of God and there is nothing. Not even space.

Allowing then that words and images are not much use, we still have to use words and images with which to form our ideas because they are the best we have got and they have been given us for this purpose. Perhaps we get closest to the idea of God's will animating his creation when we think of it as God breathing into the work he does, into the works we see and live with and are. It is the illustration which he himself chooses when he begins to reveal himself in holy scripture. He breathes life. The act of breathing is something continuous: not something switched on to meet a particular emergency. It is something largely unnoticed yet absolutely vital. If beyond a certain point we get out of breath we die. And there is this highly significant feature in the illustration: that for the lungs to breathe in they must also breathe out. Neither inhaling air nor expelling it is the whole of respiration: life needs both exercises equally. The impulse comes from God: he breathes and gives life. But the impulse must be followed up: we breathe back.

If you look up the references to breathing in a concordance you will find enough material for meditation on the will of God to last you a lifetime. Notice particularly how our Lord breathes into the dead body when he restores a life, how he breathes into the apostles when giving them their apostolic powers. Compare this with the priest breathing into the child at baptism, the bishop when confirming and conferring orders. Life comes with the will of God, and the will of God comes with life. But the beauty of it is we do not have to wait for the breathing of God's will: it is going on all the time and in every place. Our true happiness, our holiness, consists in breathing the breath of his will back to him from whom it comes.

Seeing the matter from this angle may not greatly affect our set prayers, but it should widen our concept of the function of prayer. By it we should come to a better appreciation of God's unsleeping interest in our affairs, of the loving concern which is ours for the asking—indeed which is there even if we fail to ask—and of the manner in which prayer co-operates with the work of God in the guidance of mankind. Take an example. Say you are asked to pray that the light of the Holy Spirit may direct the deliberations of a particular assembly. Suppose it is a question of an election or the passing of some important measure. You recite the required prayers and await the result. What is it that you are really expecting to happen? Do you think of it as training, by means of a combined effort of prayer, a beam of light upon the issue to be voted on—and so securing a clear pronouncement of God's will? Or do you think of it as the development of the Holy Spirit's life in the assembly, in each member of the assembly and in the body as a whole, so that when a decision comes to be made there will be a greater desire for God's will than there was before? Granted that you are ready to see God's will in the outcome anyway, you must surely be approaching the subject at a deeper level when considering it in the second of these two ways. The set form of the prayer may be the same either way you approach it, but to see the work of the Holy Spirit as an over-all influence, as the will of God becoming clearer in the measure that the voters yield themselves to it, would seem to hold more promise of fulfilment than to see it as pinpointing the agenda sheet and spotlighting the voting space.

The fact once established that God's will is the source of all that is, there should be no great difficulty in linking up human affairs with their origin. This is effected by the virtue of religion. The word 'religion' derives from the latin *re-ligo*: I bind back. Practising religion we bind ourselves back to where we belong. We have been separated from God by sin, and religion puts us right again: we rejoin our proper element. In this true environment everything speaks to us of God, everything represents God's will. The more we come to live our religion the clearer we come to hear the voice of his revelation and the quicker we become in recognising the representations of his will for what they really are.

A man is stricken with polio. It is the will of God, coming to him independently of himself and from outside. But more significantly the will of God is inside himself, inviting his co-operation with the affliction. 'You must accept it as God's will,' his friends tell him. Yes, but it is going to make a big difference how he accepts it. Must he think of it as God willing him to suffer? He can if he likes, but a more helpful emphasis is given to the trial if he thinks of God willing away inside his soul and giving him the grace to meet his polio in its true terms.

A man loses the ignition key of his car and cannot start for work. He reminds himself that it must be the will of God. 'God has planned from all eternity,' he tells himself, 'that I should lose the ignition key on this particular morning when I am in a hurry to get to the office.' There is nothing theologically wrong with this, but the stress is on the wrong thing. Better to say, 'God has willed from all eternity that I should rise to this sort of annoyance, and this is what I mean to do; my will inside myself is accordingly in line with his.' And incidentally it is the will of God that the friend to whom he telephones, asking to be picked up, should apply the same principle. The wife who is searching behind the cushions, the small son who has swallowed the key and has to see a doctor, the grandmother who is in a state about the whole affair: all can benefit spiritually in the same way.

Or take a less obvious example when it is a question not of an outward happening which indicates the operation of God's will but of a decision to be reached. A girl wonders if she has a vocation to the religious life. She feels an attraction to the cloister but the married life appeals to her too. Which does God will for her? Before we go any further in this let it be said that God's will is not going to be debarred from her if she chooses wrong, if she chooses according to self instead of according to grace. But suppose she is bent on choosing right, on choosing God's will whatever her own preference declares itself in the end to be. In the meantime she prays about it and awaits a clearer indication. Now surely in such cases of genuine doubt the way to get light is really to want God's will and nothing else. It is to identify one's human will in anticipation with the eternal will of God which, it may confidently be hoped, will emerge from the fog. So long as there exists a selfish prejudice either way, it is not in the interests of the soul to see the doubts resolved. Rather than declare his will before the soul is properly detached from self-seeking, God allows the genuine darkness to continue. Better to be in the dark about what to do next than to see what God wants and then to go in the opposite direction.

A ball is lying motionless on a table, Tip one side of the table or the other, and the ball rolls off. If the ball is to remain still, the surface on which it rests has to remain still. If in making decisions which have for their object the glory of God we incline one way or another towards self, the soul is not steady enough to receive the movement of the spirit. So in the case of uncertainty regarding vocation, the way to get light would be to mean the clause in the *Our Father* which chooses God's will. God's will in one form or another is going to be done anyway, but what the soul here is looking for is the chance of serving God's will rather than making do with God's will.

One last illustration before moving on to further argument and theory. A teaching sister is told by her superior to take over a certain class. The sister dislikes the subject, dislikes the children, dislikes the superior. But she goes ahead with it because she knows that it is the will of God for her to do so. It would be no more and no less the will of God for her if she liked the subject, liked the children, liked the superior. But though her likes and dislikes do not affect the will of God so far as the outward act of obedience goes, they may well affect her own inward response to the will of God. It is again the question of breathing in and breathing out: the dual function of the will of God.

There may be more merit in the distasteful than in the agreeable, but merit is not the final qualification. The love of God is the final qualification, and love is measured, as we have seen, by the degree to which we unite our wills with the will of God. At our judgment we shall not be asked whether we enjoyed doing the will of God but whether we did it. So long as we satisfy ourselves (and God) on the basic requirement of loving his will, which means doing it, we can safely leave the question of merit to be settled in the lobby.

'But in all these examples you have cited,' it might be objected at this point, 'the eventual outcome cannot but be the will of God. Win or lose, God's will is covered.' Of course. What we are trying to show here is that from *our* point of view we gain far more by adapting ourselves inwardly to the call of grace and *choosing* God's will although we would far rather not. We have the chance not merely of making a virtue of necessity but of perfecting the virtue whether the necessity is there or not. The bride in the *Canticle* sought for the Beloved in the streets, but he had already passed through the streets and was found ultimately in her own soul. The will of God is in the market place, the classroom, the hospital ward, the battlefield, the car-park, the cocktail party, the stadium, but unless it is recognised in the individual human soul it is a doctrine merely, or at best a theological fact. Rightly understood it can become a presence. It can be to the soul a reality compared with which all outward happenings and concrete things seem woefully insubstantial.

Ignoras te, pulcherrima—you do not know yourself, O beautiful one. What the Bridegroom is saying is that, unaware of the indwelling reality which is hers and which is the quality which makes her beautiful, she has no idea of what she really is. Until she has realised God's will within her she is not fully aware of what is going on. This is what St. Augustine means when he says, referring to the time before his conversion, 'You, Lord, were within me, and I was without.' Such a realisation is not simply an acquired knack, a twist of fancy. It is a habit of grace to be cultivated by response to grace. It means industry as well as insight, but once the point of perception is reached it makes a big difference to religion, spirituality, day-to-day prayer.

Seeing in every circumstance a pointer and reminder, the soul becomes more or less habitually conscious of the operation of God's will. Surrounding circumstances help the interior activity, the interior activity evaluates the surrounding circumstances. Though for the teaching nun we have talked about earlier there was her vow of obedience to accentuate her recognition of God's will in the work proposed, there is for everyone, vow or no vow, the same chance of recognising God's will in whatever has to be done. The ordinary sequence of events, unavoidable for the most part and a lot of them indifferent either way so far as the emotions go, speaks to us of God's design, and comes to us therefore from the planning mind of God.

Though it is true that circumstances do not shape our destiny for us, do not inevitably mould our characters, it is also true that according to what we bring to them the circumstances of our lives can be the means of either our sanctification or rejection. What we bring to them is either recognition of God's providence or rebellion against it. If we do not get in first and shape them, applying the doctrine of the will of God, there is always the danger that circumstances, applying the pressures of a materialistic world, may shape us.

More than two centuries ago a British ship was sailing far out at sea off the coast of South America. The expected rains had failed, the inhabitants of Brazil were hostile, and because the supply of drinking water on board had run out the men were dying of thirst. Desperate in their necessity they signalled to a passing ship (the account of the incident does not say whether it was Spanish or Portuguese) for enough fresh water to help them out until the rains came. To their dismay the signal came back to the British seamen instructing them to lower their buckets over the side and take as much as they wanted. Was it a joke? The message went out again, in still more urgent terms, and the reply came back to the effect that since they were surrounded by water the British should try using it. Eventually it was decided to let down an experimental bucket, which, when drawn up on deck, was discovered to contain not salt but fresh water. What the British did not know, but what was common knowledge to those who sailed those seas, was that the force of the Amazon was so powerful as to carry its waters miles beyond its mouth, rendering the sea-water harmless.

On all sides we are surrounded by an element which supports us; it is the element by which we are appointed to travel. It does not seem to afford us what we want. We look elsewhere. In our thirst for the things of God we look up at the heavens, and when no moisture comes from that quarter we complain that the heavens have dried up. We turn to the coastline, and despair of help from there. We send out signals of distress to others who are on the same sort of voyage as ourselves. When we are told what to do we think we are being made fools of. Eventually, because we have tried everything else without success, we follow our instructions and find that the solution has been there all along.

It is significant in this connection that in the *Rituale* of the Church are printed official blessings for every sort of commonplace object. The implication here is that linen, bread, bells, rooms, clothes, tools and farm implements, typewriters and handcarts can become the material means by which the soul reaches out to supernatural good. In themselves they are just inanimate creatures to which nobody pays much attention until they are needed for a particular purpose, but in the scheme of God's will they are playing a part as vehicles both of the divine purpose to man and the human response to God. It is as if the Creator is bent upon so saturating his creation with himself that creatures may assist one another in the recognition of his activity. If this should suggest a danger of pantheism (the heresy which identifies God with the universe) there is ample corrective in the thought that creatures, taken in the wrong way, can do just the reverse. The truth is that while material things are far from being split off pieces of the divine essence, as some have argued, the whole of life is so penetrated inside and out with the supernatural that wherever we turn we cannot evade God's will. Remember the psalmist's rueful acknowledgement: 'Lord, you have known me sitting and standing; you have seen into my thoughts from afar. My course you have searched out, and all my ways you have foreseen . . . whither shall I go from your spirit, whither flee from your face? If I mount into the heavens you are there; if I go down into the deep you are there too. How early soever I take wing, hiding in the utter remoteness of the sea, it will be your hand that leads me, your hand that holds me up. I told myself that perhaps darkness would cloak me about, that night would be on my side in my pleasures. But again darkness is not dark to you; the night is as daylight to your gaze. Wherever you look it is the same to you . . . for to you there can be nothing hid.'

Indeed if we turned more often to the psalmist for enlightenment we would enter more deeply into the mystery of God's will than by consulting psychiatrists and cataloguing our motivations. 'In the head of the book it is written of me,' he says in the thirty-ninth psalm, 'that I should do your will. O my God, I have desired it, and to have your law in the midst of my heart.' Notice how this bears out what we have been considering: the inward response of the human will to the outward demand of the law—and the relation between the two constituting God's will. Again and again in the psalms we get this idea of obedience to the design, the frame, the lines, the dispensations, the testimonies and justifications of God. God's word is everywhere about us, we cannot escape his truth. St. Augustine says that God's will is our 'firmament', but even this, unless

33

it is taken to mean the air we breathe, does not get us close enough to the reality. God's will is a more intimate fact than the firmament of the sky, the canopy under which all our acts are performed. God's will is the impulse of our acts, the motor power without which we could not do a thing or understand his word. It is by God's will, to quote the psalmist again, that we are 'established in his sight for ever' and can say 'blessed be the Lord from eternity to eternity. So be it.' This *fiat, fiat* with which the fortieth psalm closes can be taken to sum up all that has been said so far. Indeed if we truly mean it, our *fiat, fiat* can stand for the whole of our religious service. Practised in its perfection it defines sanctity itself.

As Fulfilled By The Saints 3

THIS is the place to examine the way in which the challenge of God's will is met by those who must be the chief exponents of the principle. In a later chapter we shall consider how our Lord fulfilled the Father's will, but for the moment our investigation takes us to those ordinary human beings like ourselves who are perfectly free to follow their own will if they want to but who in fact have chosen to follow the will of God.

For such the opening verses of St. Paul's twelfth chapter to the Romans may be representative. ''I beseech you therefore, brethren, by the mercy of God that you present your bodies a living sacrifice, holy, pleasing unto God, your reasonable service. And be not conformed to this world, but be reformed in the newness of your mind, that you may prove what is the good, the acceptable, and the perfect will of God.' The contrasting wills are shown here: the will of the world and the will of God. The soul must choose. The service of God is 'reasonable'—more reasonable actually than service of the world—and if the will of God is to be proved in its fulness there has to be an interior reformation. Forswearing conformity with the standards of the world, the truly religious soul is urged to go about the service of God in 'newness of mind'. While the body is presented as a living sacrifice, the mind is presented in the same terms—as sacrificial material. There is here the same relation that we have noted before between the outward and the inward. In the adjustment of the one to the other lies the fulfilment of the perfect will of God. Man's whole being, flesh and spirit, is the area of transformation. If one or other, human sense or human mind, is left out, then the balance is disturbed and the potential perfection is disqualified.

In case the objection is raised here that this is hardly material for beginners, it must be insisted that as a matter of fact it is. You cannot even begin unless you know what is expected of you. A saint is only a beginner who has gone deeper into the truths with which he began. There is not one law for beginners and one for experts, one spirituality for beginners and one for mystics, one will of God for beginners and another for those who are finishing. Holiness is simply the degree to which the human will is united in love to the divine, and unless we start off intending to unite our wills with God's we can never advance at all. It is a mistake to think of what the saint does in the way of service as something different in kind from what we do; the difference lies in the amount of love which he puts into it. The will of God is for all of us the same—our sanctification. How far we achieve this end will depend upon the joint forces of God's grace and our response. 'Be you therefore perfect' is addressed to all.

The proposition arrived at, then, is that we undertake some sort of reformation of heart and mind in order more perfectly to serve God rather than the world. This change is known by the Greek word *metanoia*, and by it we judge the affairs of life in a new way. They are the old affairs of life, but they are seen in new perspective. The deeper understanding of God's will insures this. In the alchemy of grace the many facets of God's will are no longer seen in diversity but in unity. As the beginner develops in his purpose he sees more and more what God's creatures represent. At the start he could acknowledge the presence of God's will only at intervals and in major events. He would read of a war breaking out somewhere, and would say to himself, 'I suppose that must be in a curious way God's will'; someone would die, and he would be forced to bow to God's will. Even for that amount of recognition there has to be a certain groundwork of *metanoia* or he would accept the purely materialist assumption that these things were of terrestrial significance only and could be accounted for without reference to a divine plan.

But then as the beginner goes to work on his *metanoia* he is brought up sharply and often by what can only be evidences of God's will. Gradually, grace working within him, the beginner looks at the world around him as a setting for the performance of God's will. He sees history as the movement of God's will. He sees sorrow, and even more mysteriously he sees sin, as part of the pattern of God's will. Where before he judged that a lot must be happening which God can scarcely have allowed for, now he can look this side of life in the face and know that nothing is going on behind God's back. He does not have to make excuses for God: he believes in the existence of a design. He may not see how things fit in, but he knows without question that they must.

So it can be appreciated that God's will is becoming comprehensive where hitherto it was piecemeal. It was comprehensive all along but the beginner did not see it so. God's will is becoming identified with God's love. They were the same thing all along but the beginner assigned to them respective operations. 'I know what is meant by the love of God,' he had said, 'because from it flow tenderness, mercy, and answers to my cry for help.' Would he have been so clear about the will of God, or would he have thought about it as something else again? Certainly if we may go by what the saints say of themselves we see a great simplicity resulting from their labours. The testimony seems universal. Whether he happens to be apostolic or mystical, intellectual or peasant, leading churchman or obscure layman, the saint is everywhere found to be a man of one idea: God's will.

Man comes to his knowledge by means of evidence from outside, by experience and practice. He does not learn all at once, but part at a time. This is true of a trade, of a skill, or of a science. People sometimes imagine that their understanding of a subject is immediate or congenital, that their talents express themselves perfectly by instinct. This is asking a lot, and short of an infused grace the abilities we possess may be claimed to have developed gradually. Even in the case of the sacraments, where the grace *is* infused, the exercise of the appropriate virtue is a matter of progressing step by step. The facility is reached, but not automatically.

Before he can get a broken down car into running order, a garage mechanic has to have picked up his knowledge from bits of metal. He has learned that certain combinations of bolts and screws and wires produce certain effects. Car maintenance is no longer a problem; he can drive without thinking. But it was not always so. Or take a musician. The composer may have a gift to start with—must have, if he is to be any good—but he learns from notes and instruments. He gets into the way of arranging isolated spots on a piece of paper so that they make up a musical score. He can finger bits of ivory, wood, metal, strings with such sureness that the required noise results. But before this can happen there have to be observation, intake, correlation. A translation has to take place inside if anything is to be expressed outwardly. A better example than either of these would be the way in which a doctor comes to treat the living human body from what he has learned as a medical student from the skeleton. The study of an object composed of many separate bones kept together by wire and hanging from a hook has given him his knowledge of anatomy. The living organism gives him far more to work on in his practice, and he is picking up new knowledge every day, but as a beginner he had to start with the bare bones, the frame.

The point is that only when the beginner has reached the stage of dealing immediately and experimentally with his material does the knowledge which he has acquired become part of him. The same is the case of the beginner with the will of God. 'This is the will of God, your sanctification,' and without man's will to sanctify himself God's will remains unfulfilled. God's will may be halfheartedly acknowledged, intermittently obeyed, but unless it evokes the kind of response which the human will is capable of rendering—'your sanctification' being possible by God's grace—there is something missing. God's will is therefore a summons. It is as though God were saying, 'Give yourself to my will, and I promise to do the rest'. From recognition, through acceptance, to identification. This is the classic sequence, the perfect service. For the will of God to come into its own as a living vitalising entity, not stopping short at the letter of the law, there have to be souls in the world who are dedicated to it. Such souls we call saints.

So when you get right down to it, what would be the attitude of mind which you would expect to find in a saint? Must it not be something which would express itself in some such form as this: 'I pledge myself wholly to the will of God, confident that whatever my obedience to its demand involves I shall not be left without the help to comply with it'? Self-surrender and trust: because these assume love, they assume everything else.

In the Old Testament the verbs 'to sacrifice' and 'to sanctify' are used to mean almost the same thing. So that when we come to the New Testament and read our Lord's prayer to the Father which contains the statement, 'for them do I sanctify myself, that they also may be sanctified in truth,' we know at once, even if we did not know what was to come in the passion, that there is here the added implication of sacrifice. Our Lord is saying more than, 'I am schooling myself to a high level of conduct so that my disciples may know how to behave'; he is saying, 'because I have surrendered myself to your will, *they* must'. What Christ wills for himself, he wills also for his disciples. 'My sacrifice, with their own sacrifices united to mine, must define the nature of Christian perfection. If they are looking for Christian holiness they must know its conditions. If they are to be sanctified in truth they must sacrifice their wills in truth. This is what I have willed for them because it is what you, Father, have willed for me. I can pay them no higher compliment than that.'

It can be judged from the terms of the commitment that not all who claim to be Christians would claim to go quite so far. Small blame to them. Truth is to be preferred to humbug. One has to begin somewhere. The question each individual has to ask himself is not, 'am I completely and irrevocably dedicated to the will of God at its highest and most taxing level?' because the answer, if honestly given, is pretty well bound to be discouraging, but rather, 'am I trying to let the will of God mean more to me?' If we can rise to the challenge of this second question we are not doing too badly; we have at least made a start. There is about the attitude at least something of a dedication. Perhaps it is only the finished product in sanctity who can answer the earlier question without blinking.

To be sanctified in truth really means *truth*. No self-deception, no hiding behind grand talk, no vaporising about a will of God which, when examined, turns out to be only one's own will with a holy label. The dedication may not be the total burnt-offering which one would like it to be, but at least it must be true as far as it goes. Confessed limitations are more pleasing to God than untrue pretensions. The practical problem becomes this: how far up the scale can the human will be pushed so that it more nearly approximates God's will for its perfection?

For answer we can look to the tenth chapter of Hebrews where the process is outlined for us thus: the law is provided by God as both the frame of our human operation and an earnest of things to come; but the law does not of itself and automatically make us perfect; something else has to be added if our service is not to stop short at exact observance; *mere* ritual purification does no more than dispose the soul; a positive reality has to be introduced, something (or better still some*one*) capable of wiping out guilt and sin and evil generally, and exercising the supremely qualifying influence for good, has to come along and the human will has somehow (which means of course by grace) to identify itself with that force, with that Person, with that will.

Then, by way of confirmation, the Epistle to the Hebrews quotes the Thirty-ninth Psalm. 'Sacrifice and oblation you did not ask for, but a body you have given me. Holocausts for sin were not enough for you. So I cried: Behold I come. The very first thing that is written of me in the book is that I should do your will, O God... then I said: Behold, I come to do your will, O God.' When Christ comes into our lives, he comes in his completeness—with his will perfectly united with the will of the Father. And when we try to come closer to Christ we come with our wills, choosing, for all our imperfection, to unite our wills with his.

It can be readily understood what an expanding influence such an attitude must exercise.

The idea is completely mistaken which makes the religious man ego-centric. The truly religious man is concerned about everything except himself. Having committed himself to God in perfect trust, he does not bother to sort himself out as he used to do. He knows that he will get farther in God's service by trust and love than by self-analysis. If there have been saints who were introspective it is not because their pursuit of holiness made them so but because they were introspective to begin with, and even their holiness did not cure them of it.

So when St. Augustine defined sanctity as 'to live by God for the sake of God alone' he was not narrowing the saint's horizon but on the contrary widening it. God's interests, which are wide enough to include the whole of his creation, are now the soul's interests. God's will, which desires the good of every single individual in the world, is reflected in the saint's attitude of wishing well to all mankind. Nor is this just a vague, all-embracing benevolence such as a naturally friendly man would feel towards his fellows, not just a warm glow such as most of us would admit to on occasions like Christmas, but rather it is the kind of charity which stands up to the test of personal self-sacrifice. The saint, because God did so in the person of Christ, goes out of his way to help and to save. He expects good to come out of sinful human beings, and where sin comes out instead he is prepared to forgive. He works towards the perfect manifestation of God's will, and where he sees rebellion against God's will he is not dismayed. He knows that divine love is stronger than human malice.

Indeed one of the mistakes which the would-be saint has to guard against is that of allowing himself to get too much upset by the evil in the world. He has to see sin and go on hating it, but he must learn to take its existence in his stride. It is related of St. Francis that in the beginning of his conversion the distress which he felt at the thought of God's love being rejected, of the innocent being corrupted, of wickedness flourishing even among those who should have been shepherding Christ's flock, was so great as to hinder him in the work he had undertaken. He expended more energy in weeping over the frailties of man than in trying to correct them. But as he advanced in holiness he came to a better balance in this matter, detaching himself from his over-tender feelings and making allowance for what God's will evidently allowed for.

So it would seem that if we are to do the work of God as apostles of his will we must avoid getting—to use your apt American phrase—'emotionally involved'. (The English, with their quaint terminology, would murmur something about not letting the windscreen-wiper run away with one.) The true apostle is confident that God has not abandoned man, and that grace will triumph in the end. To focus all attention upon vice might lead to despair; to call for the exercise of virtue is to echo the voice of God's will.

The apostle is a workman like any other. True his work is full of the grace of God, but while his feet are still on the ground he remains a realist. He can have as many ideals as he likes, the more the better, but he must go about the service of God with his sensibilities well under control. People often imagine that their love of God is outraged by the evidence of men's sins, when really it is not their love of God that is hurt so much as their nerves. Nerves, the product of a passion, must be mortified if God's work is to be done effectively. What would we think of a craftsman or labourer who allowed his emotions to dominate his job? Would we employ a decorator a second time who, having painted and cleaned up the house, came back a month later in floods of tears because he had heard we had messed up one of the walls? In the armed forces, which are rightly called 'services', a display of natural sentiment would be even more out of place. In the service of God, which is the highest employment of man, natural sentiment must give place to supernatural purpose. This means will.

The service of God—and particularly, of its very nature, the service expressed in the apostolate—involves close personal relationships. How not become committed, how remain detached? The problem is a real one, never altogether finding a satisfactory solution. But once again the answer must lie not in the deeper understanding of our own mixed motives, whose whole business it is to yield unreliable findings, but in the deeper understanding of God's will. If we truly intend to find, pursue, and perfect God's will for us in the relationships which entangle us we shall eventually come to view them within the pattern of his providence. It is only when we trust to luck that we are left to luck. Those things that we hide from God, God hides from us. Our safety lies, once more, in the realist approach: we face the issue as it is in God's sight and ask that we may come to see it as he sees it. Furthermore it must be remembered that God does not show us things as he sees them unless at the same time he gives us the grace to handle them as he wills them to be handled. What would be the point of our seeing either the danger or the solution if there was nothing we could do about it?

A certain saint (whose name I unfortunately forget) trained himself to repeat over and over again, hundreds of times a day, the clause from the *Our Father* 'thy will be done'. This practice he regarded not as a devotion but as a necessity, for whenever he left off he was assailed by the most urgent temptations against faith, chastity, and hope. As time went by he found himself reduced to a state of extreme nervous tension, rattling off ever faster and faster 'thy will be done', until he began to realise that there was an essential connection between the content of his prayer and the unsuspected nature of his temptation. Could it not be said that the Father's will *was* being done when temptation assaulted his soul? On the showing of St. James's Epistle this would seem to be the case. 'Count it all joy when you fall into divers temptations, knowing that the trying of your faith works patience…blessed is the man who endures temptation, for when he has been proved he will receive the crown of life which God has promised to them that love him.' Even if he could not go so far as to count it all joy when the attacks were raging, he could at least acknowledge the permissive and providential will of God. For an investigation of this aspect of God's will we shall need a separate chapter. It is a pity I cannot recall the identity of the saint referred to: he would surely come in useful to many. Anyway he bears out in his experience the point which we have been trying to make in this chapter.

Its Mystery 4

T HE merest glance at the history of heresies
will show that it is the will of God in one form
or another that the heretics have got wrong. In the
early Church there was the question of recon-
ciling the divine and human will in the person of
Christ. Later it was the difficulty of seeing how
the wisdom of God, which is his will just as it is
his love, operated in a Church which was composed of human beings. In Reformation times
the Protestant theologians of Germany, Switzer-
land and France, developing a much older heresy,
held that God willed some to be saved and others
to be damned and there was nothing one could
do about it. Later still there were the Quietists of
the early eighteenth century who taught that to
attain to sanctity Christians must abandon themselves so totally to the will of God as to eliminate
altogether the action of their own wills.

This is not the place for either a history lesson
or a theological exposition, but if the reader is to
get any sort of idea as to the relationship between
God in heaven promulgating his eternal will and
man on earth apparently twisting it out of all recognition, some mention must be made of the theologian's distinction between God's antecedent and

his permissive will. What beginner has not wondered at the seeming discrepancy between the doctrine of an all-wise God whose guidance is forever drawing the human race towards full stature in his divine Son and the factual indications to hand? Can wisdom itself choose unwise means to attain the required end? In going over the argument, it should be borne in mind that the term 'mystery of God's will' is a valid one. We are never going to arrive at a completely satisfactory understanding of it; but at least it will be something if we come to see the part played by human co-operation with it. Since the ground has been covered before in this series, the briefest survey will suffice here.

Working back to God from what we know of ourselves, we can trace an antecedent and a permissive way of willing in our relationships with one another. We desire, obviously, for our friends the best that life can bring. Antecedently we are willing them full happiness. While it is true that as fellow human beings we have no power to bestow this happiness upon them or make conditions for its realisation, we possess at least this much in common with God—we leave the world wide open to make its own destiny. In other words we exercise a permissive will towards those whose happiness concerns us. We feel responsible *to* them because they are objects of our love but not responsible *for* them because they enjoy their own inalienable freedom.

The parallel is lamentably inexact but bring it to bear on the infinite love which God has for

man. Antecedently he wills nothing but good.
In his love and wisdom he has given to man as his
greatest gift the power to accept or reject his will.
The liberty of the human will is that which more
than anything else makes the human soul resem-
ble the divine. So although God positively wills
one thing in the created order, he allows in that
created order which has known the Fall a different thing to happen. Had there been no original
sin the distinction would not have been necessary:
man's will would have obeyed the will of God,
would have chosen to fall in with God's designs
all along the line, and there would have been no
evil consequences to call for God's permission.
But with the rejection of willing service, man's
action is fraught with unhappy result. The so-
called problem of evil is not explained away by
this aspect of our first parents' failure but merely
made less of a mystery.

For most people the difficulty is not so much
with the existence of pain and suffering in a fallen
world as with what actually happens when the
will of God for a particular person is one thing
and the person decides to do something else.
Must this not in some way devalue God's will,
making it depend upon a perhaps purely friv-
olous decision of man's? Again an example may
serve. Assume that a devout and rich man feels
urged to build a church. He decides, after praying about it, that God wills a church to stand in a
certain area. Many Masses will be offered, Cath-
olics will be able to get to the sacraments who

would otherwise be deprived, conversions will follow and a new centre of the apostolate will be established. If this rich man were to die or lose all his money there would be no great problem. Anyone who knew about the project would assume quite naturally that it was the will of God: a pity, but manifestly the will of God. Say however the rich man stays alive and stays rich but decides to open a racing stable instead. What has happened to the will of God? There it was, all ready, and a mere man has reduced it to nothing. Death and financial loss can be regarded as acts of God, and justified accordingly, but here was an act of man. The principle remains the same in each case: the actual outcome is what God has willed, and this is far more certain than that he ever willed a church to be built in the first place. Short of a direct revelation on the subject it would not be for anyone to claim a knowledge of God's antecedent will in the matter. A point which remains open is what has happened in the mind of the rich man. Is his will now in line with the will of God? The answer must depend upon how far the undertaking had represented to him a real demand: how sincerely he had originally believed that a church was required of him. His change of plan may be anywhere between a serious rejection of grace, tantamount to turning down a clear vocation to the religious life, and a lighthearted deviation from what had been no more than a temporary religious enthusiasm. But whichever it is, and wherever he stands between these extremes, the grace is there now to help him to make the best of the circumstances as they have turned out. This is an important thing to remember, because often it is felt that once we have neglected to co-operate with God's grace at a high level we are disqualified from co-operating again. Such a view would suggest a vindictive, even a touchy God. 'All right: you have failed me over something which I wanted; now I shall cheerfully fail you over the things that you want. You have refused the heights; you can get along on the plains by yourself.'

St. Teresa at one stage lacked the generosity to accept the grace of contemplation. But by making use of the graces measured to her lower state she eventually got back to where she had been before, and higher. It took her twelve years, and though to the end of her life she was full of remorse for her early infidelity she was glad enough to have paid the price of getting back. Her experience teaches a twofold lesson: it does not pay to turn down God's offers, but if we do we have other offers waiting for us lower down the scale.

To be balanced against all this the beginner, or even the seasoned practitioner for that matter, does not have to take every noble impulse that comes to him as being the will of God. Only scruples and confusion would result. The noble impulse has to be valued in relation to surrounding circumstances. There have been instances in the lives of holy people which suggest that the interior attraction to a certain course is both so strong and so clear as to override all secondary considerations, but such occasions must be looked upon as the exception. In the ordinary way the urge, particularly if it calls for heroic or histrionic expression, must be looked at in the cold hard light of reason, against the dusty flat backdrop of actuality.

A young married couple decide that the most unselfish thing they can do is to have a mother-in-law as a permanent guest in their house. 'This is a good thing in itself, and we feel the same about it,' they argue, 'so it must be the will of God.' But must it—just like that? God will certainly bless their generosity if they follow through with the scheme, but it is equally certain that before doing so they weigh it up according to prudence. How will it affect their marriage, will it mean that the children's education will have to suffer, will friends no longer come, will arguments or example give scandal? Admittedly the main issue is the one to pray about, but these side issues may not be brushed aside as unworthy. They would not be there if they were not worthy, so God presumably wills them to act as guiding lines.

Where circumstances point in a particular direction, and still more so of course where they force a particular situation, the recognition of God's will is relatively easy. But often we have to search for God's will in a tangle of alternatives.

Our liberty of will is a great gift, but sometimes we wish we did not have so much of it. If only God, or even someone else acting in his name, would decide for us. Our job is to *discover* (in the strict sense of uncovering, and so bringing to light what is already there) God's will in the exercise of our freedom, not to *produce* it by sleight of hand from an opinionated self.

Even in the religious life, where obedience might be thought to take care of everything, it is only too possible to make the will of God seem anything but what it is. The deluded religious can manoeuvre, fooling himself and other people. It is also true that however pure his motives, the religious can be as much at the mercy of his mistaken judgment as can the layman. Is he to accept, for instance, a position of authority which is offered him but not imposed? Say he genuinely believes himself to be unequal to it. Is he wasting a chance of furthering God's work for souls by playing safe, or is he taking the reasonable means of averting disaster? Ought he to make the supreme act of trust in God's grace and go ahead, or does God want him to use his freedom of will to back out while the backing is good? Neither circumstances nor the opinions of others tell him everything. His own judgment and his own experience may yield no information. What is he to do? There is nothing else he can do but pray. If he prays with a detached heart, it does not matter which alternative he chooses. If he really wants only the will of God he cannot miss it.

Indeed if he really prays he has got it already, before he makes the choice.

Accordingly if we are sincere when we say in the *Our Father* 'hallowed be thy name' we are pronouncing an earnest of the next clause, 'thy kingdom come'. An earnest also of the one after, 'thy will be done on earth as it is in heaven'. These three prayer acts, whether regarded as acts of praise or petition, are not entirely eschatological in their implication. They can be applied to the immediate and temporal just as they can be applied to the general and eternal. 'Hallowed be thy name' in the Chinese rendering of the *Our Father* becomes 'may all men do homage to thy name as holy'. By looking toward a time when living people universally worship, the soul is both assuming the power of God and begging the power of God to bring it about. There is nothing humanistic about this regard for the perfection of mankind on earth: the concern is that all men may unite with the activity of grace, and so give perfect worship to God. Back once more to the breathing in and breathing out. Granted that God's spirit informs the human soul, the human soul can breathe the prayer of the blessed in heaven and mean all that 'hallowed be thy name' implies.

Another facet to the subject, and one which has margins of contact with those considered above, is the Quietist misconception mentioned already. Without adopting an heretical position, people can take the view that if God's will is always present in their lives, doing its perfect work anyway, the best thing is to let it run on without any help from them. The direction here is straight towards fatalism.

As propounded originally by the circle of mystics and recollects, the tenets of Quietism looked innocent enough. Indeed they looked highly spiritual and sanctifying. The human will must be so wholly surrendered to God's will that it desires nothing, hopes for nothing, does nothing except under the direct action of grace. Nothing much wrong with that. But in fact it was heading for supine inertia. 'God's will' became a fetish; man's will became a cipher. Orthodoxy would have been preserved had a measure of human co-operation been demanded, but co-operation was held to be quite enough in the way of operation to spoil the work of God. The soul was required not to transform self but to annihilate self. Prayer for the Quietist was not just a matter of keeping the emotions still so as to simplify the act of the will; it was a matter of eliminating activity of any sort, whether of the emotions or of the will.

Madame Guyon was to write of the soul perfected by grace that 'it is as little possible for it to distinguish itself from God as God distinguishes himself from it'. On such a showing the human individual, when made holy, has no longer any real existence of his own. He is not an entity working for the fulfilment of God's will, he is not even a passive instrument wanting to be used: he is a vacuum, an emptiness. If God cannot distinguish himself from such a soul he is clearly not the God of Christian teaching. At least the Quietist errors had this effect: they showed us the necessity of using our wills *as* wills. The highest thing a human will can do is freely to will God's will.

If this means anything at all it means that there must be occasions in life when it is not enough to sit back and wait for God's will to roll over one. There are times when, for the very fulfilment of God's will, the initiative has to be taken. In the event the action may prove to have been misplaced or untimely, but this is not to say that it ought never to have been taken. 'It is God's will,' says Bossuet, 'that we should do nothing listlessly', and one of the dangers of too much abandonment is that we come to do everything listlessly. How not—if we feel guilty about doing anything at all?

Any school of spirituality which jettisons the moral autonomy of man, even if it is in the name of giving greater glory to God, is bound to fall foul of Catholic teaching. For us the way of giving glory to God is by being ourselves—by willing and acting in harmony with the vocation which God has given us. Such action is free and individual. If we so sacrificed our liberty to choose God's will we would be machines and would give only a mechanical glory to God. If we so sacrificed our individuality as to become merged in a kind of general human fluid where would be the doctrine of a personal redemption?

Though the theology of Quietism is dead, the Quietist way of thinking is very much alive. More alive now, since the arrival upon our horizon of nuclear weapons of destruction, than twenty or thirty years ago. People imagine it to be a virtue to wait upon the will of God long after the will of God has been suggested to them. There is no merit in passivity as such. '*Do* unto others,' our Lord says, 'as you would have them do unto you.' He speaks about positive undertakings more often than about getting out of the stream of life. Talents must be traded with, wheat must be sown and harvested, leaven must spread. 'I have finished the work,' he was able to say at the end, 'thou gavest me to *do*.' 'Indeed this was the Son of God,' it could be said of him when he had finished; 'he did all things well.'

We have to do more than merely accept the evil in the world; we have to resist it. Yet to judge from a trend in present day spiritual writing, stagnation is better than sticking one's neck out. Are we never to initiate, but always to allow other people's initiations to dominate? Are we never to reform, but always to assume that God's will is directed against change? Are we never to correct offenders on the grounds that offences are the due expressions, in a fallen world, of God's permissive will? Put in these terms the way of passive endurance may look ridiculous, but there is not a very clear line of demarcation between the passive endurance which is of God and that which is sheer sloth. It would be sad if we of this period in history, of all periods, evaded our responsibilities because of a muddle-headed understanding of the will of God. More will be said about this in the concluding chapter.

If the doctrine of conformity to God's will is to mean invariable acceptance of the existing order then it would be imperfection ever to change anything at all. A soul would do wrong to change from the lay state in order to enter religious life, a single person would have to stay single because such was the state to which he happened to belong. But God's will not only allows for changes but often demands them. It is likely to demand a number of significant changes as the result of the Second Vatican Council, which itself would never have been convened were the *status quo* to be infallibly identified with God's will.

It is perhaps typical of our age that people enjoy the hunt more than they enjoy the find. It is a commonplace to observe how useless is the pursuit of leisure if people do not know what to do with their leisure when they have got it. It would seem to be the same with regard to the will of God: people talk a lot about it, and are forever harping upon how assiduous they are in the search for it, yet when the will of God is shown them they look the other way. Important as search and expectation are, they are not to be rated above performance.

A few months ago I was sitting in a doctor's waiting-room in Bristol. Also waiting were two other men, neither of whom I knew. One was reading back numbers of *Country Life*; the other, too agitated to read, was restlessly moving about and looking at his watch. After a while this second man came over to where I was sitting, and said this: 'Everyone gets ill at some time or another. I've been ill before, and I've known it was all part of the day's work. But this time it's the wrong illness.' Then, since I had no comment to make, he added 'and it's come at the wrong time.' The other man, without looking up from his *Country Life* and showing no sign that he had heard, said, 'but to the right person'.

If we believe in the providence of God it is always the right person who gets the right expression of God's will. If there is mystery in much connected with the subject there is nothing but straightforwardness here. However straightforward the principle, even however blatently obvious the manifestation, there is always the obstacle of what might be called escapeful thinking. When presented with the occasion we look for a way round it, for a way out. Our view of God's will is bi-focal: long-sightedly we see it coming, near-sightedly we fail to recognise it.

It is a curious thing that while we in America and England are more free than most with our counsels of perfection we are noticeably reluctant to follow them to their conclusions. Historians may well point to this era as one in which the religious idea was matter for popular discussion. But if all this enquiry does not have the will of God as its aim, it might just as well not be going on. People will tell you airily they are searching for truth, and if you talk to them about God's will they object that you are being too narrow. If they are looking for a truth which is 'broader' or 'more objective' or 'more scientific' than 'religious' truth, it is not surprising that they miss truth itself when they come across it. The truth of God is the will of God, as it is also the love and the power of God, and unless it is sought on its own terms it is mistaken in the substitutes which men have made for it. The will of God may contain a mystery, but there is all the difference in the world between a mystery and a confusion.

The Test **5**

THE response of the human will is easily tested. It is simply a question of whether we make, to the point of acting on it, the divine will our own or whether the words 'thy will be done' are no more than a presumed passport.

You may object that even this fails as a touchstone because it is by no means clear what is meant by 'making God's will one's own'. All right, by way of explanation we can again draw upon the relationship between two people who are fond of one another.

When a husband or wife says, 'leave my wishes out of this: you should know by now that in marrying you I made your happiness more important than my own,' we have a reasonably clear idea of what is implied. Such a remark must, if it is sincere, come from a heart which is not greedy for its own satisfaction. There has been self-giving here; there has been recognition not merely of another's rights as a married person but of something else which, though obviously suggested by the marriage vow, is not explicitly demanded in the contract. The handing over has been complete. 'Whatever makes you happy, that I choose. As far as I am concerned alternatives no

63

longer present themselves: I follow a single course—the one which pleases you.'

In man's relationship with God the situation is much the same. By implication the Christian is committed to what pious books used to call the 'goodpleasure' of God. The graces of baptism are such that they destine the soul which makes proper use of them to the highest holiness and to the fulfilment of God's goodpleasure. The Christian obligation admits of a minimal service but it calls to a maximal one. Just as a married person, by satisfying his responsibilities and not being unfaithful, is honouring the requirements of marriage, so the Christian, by trying to keep out of mortal sin, is fulfilling the letter of the law. Such a Christian is obeying the will of God, but he can hardly be said to have made God's will his own. He is not putting God's *goodpleasure* first.

To 'make God's will one's own' is accordingly to establish a single criterion. It is to forget about rights and personal inclinations: it is to look only to one guiding principle. On the negative side it is to discount prejudice, worldly standards of judgment, material advantage; on the positive side it is to make love the final arbiter. When the human will has surrendered to the divine will as fully as this, then God's purpose in creating the soul has been achieved and life for that soul assumes balance and order; until such a surrender has taken place, balance and order are uncertain. (This point will be developed in a later chapter when the effects of conformity to God's will are examined.)

When St. Paul urges the Corinthians to 'do all their works in charity' this is exactly what he means. If they love the will of God more than they love their own wills, they must inevitably be doing works of charity all day long. They will be willing what is best, they will be loving God and their neighbour in the ordinary things they have to do. And the things that are done to them, whether bringing joy or sorrow, will be received in charity. Having chosen God's will in everything, they see everything as evidence of God's will.

In the Eighty-third Psalm the sacred writer expresses this interaction between the human and the divine will. 'My heart and body have rejoiced in the living God…blessed is the man whose help is from you, O God, for in his heart he has purposed to mount by the degrees appointed …the lawgiver shall bestow his blessing, and they shall go from virtue to virtue…better is one day in God's house above thousands. I have chosen to be abject in the house of my God, rather than to dwell in the tents of sinners.' The soul has made the choice of God's will in preference to temporal pleasure, so it can rejoice in being abject if abjection is the state God bestows. God is the lawgiver, and whatever comes from the lawgiver, be it pleasing or painful, is a blessing. Those thus blessed go, inevitably, from virtue to virtue: God's help, which is his will, goes with them.

The serious choice of God's interests in preference to self-interest involves a considerable reorientation. It means that self's whole interest is pleasing God. Self is pushed out of the picture. Nor can self, still looking round for satisfaction as it will go on doing without willing to, claim any great merit for what seems so heroic a choice. Self recognises the full truth of our Lord's words 'you have not chosen me, but I have first chosen you'. In the practical order the change of focus is found to make a great difference. It means that instead of serving God in the way we think he ought to like, we serve him in any way we can —which will be the way he wants. We let God choose the way. Instead of putting our confidence in various practices of prayer, penance, charity and so on which we have devised for ourselves, we shall be putting our confidence in his handling of our lives. What we would draw up in the way of a scheme or rule of life may objectively look far more 'perfect' than what in fact is required of us by God's will. But 'perfection' now denotes only one thing, God's will. When the soul has surrendered to all that is God's will there is no longer any need to bother about different interpretations of perfection.

A would-be saint cannot always be certain that extra fasting is going to please God, but he can always be certain that self-surrender will. Hours spent in prayer *may* be a form of self-indulgence; surrender to God's will can never be. It is the substitution of the whole for the parts, it is directing attention to the end instead of to the means. The service of God is not to be restricted to performance; it looks to the attitude of mind and heart. Outward execution follows the inward actuation; it is no substitute for the activity of the will. When a man's will is united with the will of God the acts which he performs flow from a more significant source than ingenuity in devising a form of service.

People, and especially beginners in the spiritual life, so often mistake the theoretical and idealised will of God for the actual. A girl for instance will judge that the most perfect thing for her to do is to leave the world and become a nun. In the counsels of perfection there is every justification for this: 'If thou wilt be perfect' our Lord said, 'sell what thou hast, give to the poor, and follow me.' But the point is it may not be the vocation for *her*. She has been right to judge that she is called to perfection, but mistaken in judging that the convent life was to be the setting for it. She makes a trial of the life and after a period of trial comes away. The test of her essential vocation is still going on, and is perhaps more searching now than when she entered the novitiate. What is her attitude now towards the will of God? Much will depend upon whether she looks back with resentment or with gratitude; whether she looks forward trusting to luck or believing in God's providence. She can say either 'the whole thing was a delusion: I was a fool to aim at perfection: I gave myself to God, and he has shown that he does not want me: in future I make no offers, thank you, and will follow my own will,' or, as she is being given the grace to say, 'I went in because I thought it was the will of God: I can assume therefore that although he did not mean me to persevere he did mean me to try: I came out because it was God's will that I should: all I have to do now is to find out what kind of perfection he wants from me, and where I can best realise it: what I want above all is his satisfaction: my happiness is his will, and his glory is my will.'

It may be inferred that in the more strictly interior order of prayer the same principle will apply: there will be either confusion and discouragement, followed perhaps by the decision to give up praying altogether, or there will be abandonment in faith to the purpose of God. In the beginning there may have been all sorts of preconceived ideas as to how prayer ought to be made, as to what it would feel like when going properly, as to the stages which might be expected in the advance towards the higher mystical transformations. Then, in the actual experience of prayer, comes something quite different. The question is now, as it was in the case of the girl who had a vocation to try her vocation but whose true vocation was to something she had not thought of, which way will the soul jump? Is it to be: 'I should never have started on the course of prayer: it was not for me: if I want to serve God, I must find some other way: this experience has been a stumbling-block to my faith'? Or is it to be: 'I have no ideas about prayer any more: I am incapable of practising the methods suggested: I want to praise God in my prayer but I find I cannot do it; I do not know the meaning of love: all I know is that if God wills this state for me, a state which seems a waste, I will it too: his will means more to me than my spiritual satisfaction or sense of security: his will is my whole desire'? If the ultimate test is looked for, this is it.

In case some may see in this doctrine of substituting God's will for one's own an alienation of something which we have no right to alienate, it would be as well to clear up the point before taking on anything else. The whole weight of the argument rests on the fact that man only really begins to live when he has begun to die to self. Far from being contemptuous of human freedom the theory sees true human freedom as being realised only when the human will surrenders itself wholly to the divine. So it is not so much an abdication as an initiation. There is here no loss to human personality but rather infinite enrichment.

The reason why most people are unsure of themselves is because they have never properly found themselves in the context of God's will. If all men made it their first objective to discover God's will and live by it they would not only find for themselves the individualities which God meant them to have and develop but also help to create the environment which God meant them to have and develop. God's will would then be standard throughout the world: standard not in the sense of a force compelling regimentation, but in the sense of grace and truth inviting co-operation. It is only because man's final purposes and immediate endeavours become so overshadowed by what *he wants* that they drift farther and farther away from the providential scheme. The wider the gap, the more difficult it is for the individual human being to see the relationship.

Hence the many confusions in the world. If the connection between God's will and man's true interest were seen, how could there be any problem about civil rights, nuclear war-heads, aid to starving peoples? But since the connection is not seen, the remedies applied are at best social and humanitarian. Man is made in the image and likeness of God, and when this fact is overlooked everything takes on a humanist character. So of course there is chaos. Where the source of human justice is left out of account, and the justice of God is his love, the human aptitude for injustice has only human uprightness to oppose it. In a fallen human race, the natural virtues, left to themselves and divorced from supernatural grace, are not enough.

So for humanity at large, as for its individual members, the main trouble is that of not finding its destined place in the plan of God. Since we are here concerned more with the particular than with the general, we must get back to the soul's search for its true identity. This is a personal thing, a unique adventure in every case, so it will be more by prayer than by argument and study that any progress towards truth-in-self and self-in-truth will be made. What follows is given rather as an incitement to pray than in proof of a thesis.

'A man must live his own life.' This statement may be made by way of excuse, authorisation, correction, sympathy. It is not on any showing a very original reflection. But however superficial there is an inwardness to the pronouncement which deserves a closer look. A man *has* to live his own life and nobody else's. A man has to *live*, and not merely put in time until he dies. A man has to come to terms with the life he is given, however dull or disagreeable the setting, whatever his aspirations to a nobler life, wherever the direction of his main interests.

In *The Shoes of the Fisherman* Mr. Morris West makes one of the characters, a journalist, say, 'I'm not a man; I'm just a name in a suit. There's no me at all. One push, and I fall apart.' You meet that man every day; he is all over the world. You cannot even push him because there is nothing to push. There is no resistance to pressure. It is easier to help a strong character who is wrong than a weak one who is right. Why are there so many—why are perhaps we ourselves—like Mr. West's fictional character? (Though it should be added that the character in the novel shows himself to be of tougher quality than his self-appraisal suggests.) Is it not because in order to be yourself you have to be the person God means you to be, and if you are not that person you are nothing? There is every justification for the present-day cult of the unhero: it is the attempted justification of ourselves. If we refuse to unite ourselves with the will which has created us for a specific purpose we are rudderless creatures. Clinging to our own cherished images of ourselves we sacrifice substance. If we surrendered ourselves to the true image which God has of us, frankly accepting the discrepancy between the reality of God's will and the dream we have created for ourselves, we would be not only holier and happier but also more of a help to other people. When what they want to lean on is something solid, how can people be helped by what is itself leaning on unreality? There can be no support but in truth, and there is no truth apart from God's will. We find our identity only in God.

It is a characteristic of the young to indulge in hero worship. Nature has arranged that they should. If the small boy of six did not admire his father and try to imitate him, there would be something wrong either with the small boy or with the father. At a later stage in growing up, during the period of adolescence and perhaps for a while after it, admiration and imitation go out to those with whom there may be no personal relationship and who may even be complete strangers. All this is a part of education. Standards are not always conveyed by means of the spoken or written word, nor do they always come from the constituted authority. The impact may be made through example, appearance, mannerism, a particular ideal which is felt to be important. All this is perfectly normal but if it is to be productive of good there are two conditions to be satisfied: the hero must possess qualities which are worth admiring; the admirer must retain his own personality. If the one admired is shallow the influence is not likely to last; if he has character but no principles the influence will be malign; if he has character and principles, and at the same time does not want to absorb the other's individuality, the influence is almost bound to be good. *Almost*, because the other person's attitude must be taken into account. However admirable the hero is, and this would be true even if the hero is a saint, the admirer is a person in his own right and may not become a carbon-copy—even of a saint. Moreover if he, the admirer, continues to model himself on someone else when he is no longer in the formative stage of normal development he will remain forever immature. He will not be the integrated person God means him to be. He will belong neither to God nor to himself. He will be just a shadow.

In order to reach maturity, then, it is important not to get lost in someone else's maturity. True maturity is being oneself as a child of God. Many religious people make this mistake of taking up some saint and trying to mould themselves to the shape. But what if the shape is not the one which God has designed? No two shapes are alike. All souls are made for God, but each goes by a unique way. Each has to decide whether to surrender to something less than God—and so becoming if not a slavish imitation a diminished person—or to surrender to the will of wisdom itself and finding identity and freedom.

Take the case of an ordinary humble man who does not know what to do with his life, who lacks confidence, who sees his contemporaries getting ahead of him and who judges that his own lack of success must be traced to want of personality. He is no longer a boy; there is no hero to whom he can attach himself. So he follows one project after another, stirring up enthusiasm for each, but never seems to find himself in any of them. He remains, to draw from the jargon of the moment, self-consciously 'unfulfilled'. Anyone can see he is unfulfilled. True, it may be in the design of God that to go through life like this in fact fulfills the divine purpose, and that our man with the missing personality is discovering a secret personality known only to God. If this is so it can only be because the will of God has been accepted, and that in drifting from one thing to another the misfit has deliberately fitted himself in to the providential design. (And this of itself would show that personality is present in abundance.)

Normally, however, a man is meant to find his vocation and himself in the life which declares itself. The vocation to be a misfit must be a rare one. Those who are restless and dissatisfied, ever questing and wanting to better themselves, are mostly too preoccupied with themselves to think about the will of God and the vocation to follow it in full perfection. Theirs are haphazard lives with scarcely any Godward direction. Projecting themselves into one role after another they finally project themselves into the role of failure.

There is nothing wrong with failure when it comes as a grace from God but it is not something to be opted for and dramatised. A false identification with God's will, whether by assuming it must always be what one wants it to be or by expecting it always to be calamitous, leads only to unreality. What is real in a man's character, and consequently what is real in his experience, can come to light only in so far as it is related to the truth—to reality itself as it exists in God. Without God in his life, man is submerged. He lies under an ocean of self and sin and uncertainty, always trying to see the sky but unable to because of the waters which come between. There is only one way of rising to the surface, and then the sun does the rest.

All this is not an attempt to provide a simple, cellophane-wrapped remedy for nervous, psychological, and emotional disorders. It has a more positive purpose. It is intended to encourage souls to make the supreme act of trust. It is not to claim in romantic terms that, having done so, they will then be 'launched upon the grand adventure of their lives' and that from now onwards they will have nothing to do but observe the smooth and beautiful wisdom with which God handles their affairs; rather it is to claim that in the blood, tears, and confusion of life there will be something to cling onto which nothing can possibly disturb. The psalmist knows all about this when, having just complained of the darkness in himself, he prays in the 142nd Psalm: 'Teach me to do your will, for you are my God. Your own good spirit shall lead me into the right land; it is you who brings my soul out from trouble.'

Its Effects 6

H<small>AVING</small> cautioned against expecting a panacea, we can now examine some of the consequences which should in fact follow the commitment to God's will. The first and most noticeable result of entrusting ourselves to the goodpleasure of God must surely be a sense of security and relief. In pledging ourselves to divine wisdom we no longer fear the outcome of our decisions, no longer doubt the value of our trials, no longer have misgivings on the score of wasted effort. We come to know beyond all question that we know nothing about our lives and that God knows all. This being so, it is with absolute confidence that we hand over the whole direction of affairs to him.

Does this smack of fatalism, abrogation of personal responsibility, smug detachment? No, not so long as we go on willing and so long as we go on working as though everything depended on our effort. There is a vast difference between 'I needn't bother any more; I've made the supreme act' and 'I've made the act, and to prove it I'll go on trying just as hard; but what happens as a result is not my business.' It is the difference between sacrificing freedom and sanctifying freedom—a distinction which may not have been appreciated in the Old Testament use of the almost synonymous words 'sacrifice' and 'sanctify' but which is amply accounted for in the tradition of the New.

Freed at last from laocoonizing itself in a tangle of mixed motives, the soul which has surrendered to *whatever* God wills can meet the serpents one by one. No matter what God asks, no matter how complicated life becomes, no matter where our inclinations lie, no matter the degree of utter exhaustion to which we have been reduced, all we need to be clear about is that God's will is somehow coming through. This is the one thing that assumes any importance. The scale of values has now altered, and there is no longer room for —in the strict sense—disappointment. Incongruity is ruled out because an exact balance, according to this world's estimate, is not expected. Everything, even injustice and the suffering of the innocent, is assumed to have a reason. The ordinary stumbling-blocks to faith are stumbling-blocks no more but rather mounting-blocks.

Accordingly the anxieties which are common to most of us tend to lessen. We now stand in the words of the *Benedictus*, 'to serve him without fear, in holiness and equity,' because those things which threaten our happiness must be powerless against a happiness which consists in willing the happiness of God. An unhappy man is nearly always one who lives under the shadow of some dread. The present opportunity of enjoying life is darkened because he is all the time steeling himself to meet a horror in store. He is afraid he may have to go into hospital or retire from his job; he fears the death of someone he loves; he fears financial loss, atomic war, old age, death. Perhaps the fear is more subtle and what he is afraid of is happiness or love. Or perhaps he fears the sheer continuance of his unhappiness—whether he knows the cause of it or not. Well, all this is at least made bearable, though possibly not much more than that, when underlying it is seen to be the will of God. It is made more positively worth while when embraced as the will of God and offered to the greater glory of God. Even failure in marriage, failure in vocation and aspiration, failure in being able to adjust to existing conditions—all the countless failures which normally engender fears and are engendered by fears—can be resolved in the context of God's love. 'Perfect love casts out fear', but even a love which is imperfect goes a long way.

Man is not required to see the end, temporarily speaking, to which his experiences are leading him. Far better that it should be hidden from him. He can guess if he likes, but he will nearly always be wrong. If, however, he makes as the end of all he experiences a realisation beyond human existence then he acts sensibly; then he acts in faith. The sort of happiness he is now envisaging 'neither the rust nor the moth can consume' and it lies beyond the reach of robbers who might steal it away from him. Man can never entirely rid himself of fears, anxieties, depressions, because his emotions have to be taken into account and these will go on disturbing him however well ordered the rational side of him has become.

Emotional disturbances can be the lot even of the saints. Sanctity is not proof against mind-body pressures. Instinctive reflects, compulsions, chain-reactions: these things go on bothering people far advanced in holiness. The difference is that where holy people make allowance for them and keep them in their place, we do not. We let them get on top of us. We let them escape from the frame of God's will and so assume new menace. It might be thought, for example, that to be habitually in a state of grace would ensure a state of contentment. 'If I keep out of the occasions of sin, surely I am entitled to peace of mind?' You are not *entitled* to anything, and your mistake lies in equating the spiritual with the emotional.

It is true that spiritual, moral, and emotional problems react on one another. But they still remain problems after the main problem, union of the will with the will of God, has been resolved. And they remain separate. If a person of spiritual aspirations decides upon a course of moral lapses, he will experience conflict. This is obvious. But even when he has got his conduct under control again, and is willing what God wills, his emotions may well tend to run off and give him cause for anxiety and upset. Though on rational and spiritual grounds he has no call to worry, nervously and emotionally he may feel himself being torn apart. We shall have occasion to return to this point when considering the mind of Christ under pressures similar to our own.

Viewing the subject positively, from the standpoint of what help true spirituality can bring, we can judge that objectively material remedies can take on a spiritual character when accepted as the will of God. Whether a man is suffering from mental or physical ills, he can make use of the natural curative forces in full confidence that they are a means ordained by God. If God's will traces the pattern of a man's life, then it can be taken to have provided the natural as well as the supernatural equipment for the ordering of that life. Grace, particularly the grace which comes through the sacraments, performs its therapeutic work upon the soul. If mind and body have their appropriate therapies, the discoveries of medical science still owe their origin to God. Most of us tend to dwell too much upon the fact that God afflicts us with diseases and not enough upon the fact that he also sends remedies to relieve them. If one lot represents God's will so does the other.

But whatever we say about God's will and health, our main concern here is with God's will and happiness. Whether you call it happiness or peace of mind, you come to know the quality at a more significant level by union with its source than by anything else. Assuming that your religious objective is not the elimination of anxiety, nor even ridding yourself of temptation, you may stake your security on surrendering everything to the unqualified will of God. You lose your life in order to find it, and if you do not put your reliance upon the truth of this paradox there is no knowing where else you can put it. Nothing carries such gilt-edge guarantees.

A further consequence of abandonment to the will of God is detachment. This is not quite the same as what we have been discussing above, peace of mind, but it arrives at the same thing in the end. Someone who is centred on God is, and to that extent, de-centred from self. People can become so fascinated by the complexities of their lives, the multiplicity of their desires, the permutations of their daydreams, that they come to miss the one thing which really matters. God's will is the unifying factor in life, the universal denominator which brings simplicity, and when people try to bypass it they must necessarily find themselves encumbered with every sort of complication. A holy indifference to self's ceaseless clamour for what is either of secondary importance or of no importance at all is one of the first signs that a soul has made everything over to God.

Those who belong to the world naturally want to accumulate as much of what the world has to offer as they can lay their hands on. Those who are dedicated to a science, an art, an ideology in such a way as to exclude interest in other fields are going to end up, unless they are careful, with an obsession. Those who make even of religion such an exclusive and intensive pursuit that they will override social and natural demands can become victims of delusion and religious mania. Unfortunately we can make an obsession of almost anything. *Almost* anything. It is difficult to see how the will of God can become an obsession, but if it can it must only be because the doctrine has been misunderstood.

Rightly understood the doctrine detaches from obsessions, extravagances, failures of right emphasis. Once someone has allowed himself the luxury of a mania, he has placed himself at the mercy not only of sane circumstance (which is always likely to interfere with his eccentricities) but also of attacks which his own mind has exaggerated. To entertain an obsession is, by definition, to put things in false perspective. The over-valuation of a part spells impoverishment to the whole. At first other parts get neglected and ultimately the whole balance is lost. What this is leading up to is that God's will lies in the whole of a thing just as it lies in its parts, and to give the undue emphasis of an obsessive attention to one or other of the parts is a selective act which cannot be said to conform with God's will. It is a denial of the wholeness of God's will. It is an expression of self and not of service. *And* it is doomed to disappointment.

Obsessions are doomed to disappointment for this reason: though they are chosen very often by the will, they reside mostly in the imagination. The imaginary is highly vulnerable. Whether you let yourself become obsessed by health, food, money, sleep, time, silence, speed, sex, clothes, religious observance or any of the hundred preoccupations that draw the mind to a pinhead point of focus, you let yourself at the same time become a prey to the imaginary persecution, the imaginary neglect, the imaginary criticism, envy, ridicule, suspicion and the rest. You no longer see things in proportion. You cannot, because you do not see them as God sees them. In order to see them as God sees them you have to detach yourself from your obsessions and attach yourself to the will of God. Once you *have* attached yourself to the will of God, you see at least enough of truth to make your exaggerations look childish.

We are not talking now about the perfectly legitimate concern which a parent should feel for the morals of the young, which a religious superior should feel for the spirit and observance of the community, which a missioner should feel for the spread of the Faith. Concern of this sort goes with responsibility and is healthy. Its absence would point to lack of either feeling or zeal or both. But because there is here no obsession there is also no panic. When the parent, superior, missioner finds he is being stampeded into panic it is time for him to question himself on his attitude towards the will of God. Though serenity does not always prove the possession of the supernatural point of view—because the godless too can be serene—panic cannot but betray a want of trust.

Take the panic, for instance, occasioned by

scruples. Scruples come from a false conscience. What happens is that the imagination fastens on some aspect of sin, and exaggerates it out of all proportion to reality. Sin comes to be seen everywhere; the soul is obsessed with it. The soul is not looking for God's will, but for justification of its own groundless anxiety. It is looking so restlessly for relief that the will of God is not clearly seen. Since scruples are founded upon a process of reasoning which is invalid they can be stilled only when the soul has submitted to truth. Once the human will has accepted as valid the reasoning which is imposed by obedience, in the place of that imposed by the imagination and a false conscience, the panic ceases. Why? Because the soul has accepted the will of God.

If obedience is difficult for the scrupulous person, and common sense useless to him for the time being, the virtue of trust is the way back to sanity. Trust in God's providence and in his mercy will lead to trust in the representatives of his will. Without the exercise of this confidence, expressed in submission to another's judgment, the trial of scruples can bring a soul to the verge of desperation. Often it is easier to bow to God's will in a disaster such as a death than in the word of an authority. God is not tied to a particular mode of communication, and for those who are blinded either by the shock of loss or by a conflict of opinion in a matter of obedience, there is always just enough light to see what is wanted. We know what he wants. He wants our surrender.

If the picture seems fanciful and far-fetched it at least illustrates what should happen when the human will tries to unite itself with the divine will and to see life from God's point of view. The mind comes to see unity in diversity, comes to experience the real meaning of simplicity. You get the idea in the canticle *Benedicite* from the prophecy of Daniel and in the *Laudate* psalms. All the separate works of God's creation—sea, mountains, rivers, animals, people, angels—come together in the single act of worship and submission to God's will. However scattered it looks, everything in the world fits in. Everyone with his own private personal history merges with the history of mankind, with the history of God's providence.

Nothing, moreover—to return to the fairy-tale theme—is in the strictest sense 'lost'. If it goes astray it can always be found again. It can be restored to where it belongs. The American term is perhaps better here: the office represents the lost *and* found. There is a place for everything, even for the stray. Even those who are not in a state of grace and who have no intention of saving their souls are, though in a somewhat oblique way, fulfilling the will of God. God has not had that purpose in mind—that they should rebel against him—but the fact that they have used their freedom to choose, even though they have chosen wrong, is witness to his will.

In one of the sapiential books we read of God's wisdom as 'reaching from end to end mightily

Here is a theme if anyone wants to write a fairy-story or a ballet. The scene is a lost-property office (I believe that it is called in America a lost-and-found department) and the time shortly before midnight on Christmas eve. Every sort of object is lying about, the more portable on shelves and the unwieldy in heaps and against the wall. Umbrellas, bicycles, suitcases, bird-cages, parcels, hats, wheel-barrows, rocking chairs, toys, pieces of Greek statuary, baskets of decaying fruit and vegetables. As the clock over the entrance strikes twelve, the doors open and every object flies out on its way back to its owner.

To us there is the element of mystery and fantasy because we have no idea to whom the objects belong, and we are kept guessing as to how they are finding their way home. God, looking down from heaven upon such an assortment, knows exactly to whom each object belongs, when it came into their possession, when and where it got lost, what journey would be involved in the flight to restoration. To us all these things are unrelated to one another: therein lies their surrealist charm. But to God there is a pattern, and every single pair of glasses, every old deflated football, every china vase has its own special associations and its own place in the general scheme. There is nothing incongruous in a telescope lying next to a frying-pan—not more incongruous than a lion lying next to a lamb or the leopard next to the kid. There is intimate harmony between all these separate things, and God sees them unified in the unity of his will.

With regard to charity in relation to God, thought of simply as worship, identification with the divine will assumes both the desire to give glory and the actual execution. Whether the prayer which the individual soul feels it to be God's will that he should practice is vocal or mental, distracted or clear, private or public, the principle holds good equally: the intention is to serve God's will. If the intention looks more to the individual's will than God's, then the charity in the prayer is to that extent lessened. It is clear that those who take the precept in its fullest sense and seriously set themselves to love the Lord their God with their whole heart, mind, and soul have already envisaged God's will and admitted it into their lives. Just as in God his will and his love are one, so in us the response to his will is the measure of our love.

Turning now to the other aspect of charity, love of neighbour, we can apply our earlier conclusions about the unity and simplicity of God's purpose. The theme of the *Benedicite* and *Laudate* of the Old Testament is repeated for us, and in the warmer terms of human relationship, in the New. From our Lord himself we get the symbols of the vine, the flock, the field, the net: each one showing the work of the unit within the whole; each one illustrating the corporate nature of sanctification. In the epistles we have St. Paul teaching the same doctrine: different members of the one body working together for the life of the whole; a diversity of gifts but the same spirit;

and ordering all things with gentleness'. Nothing is so mightily commanded that liberty gives way to compulsion; nothing is so gently arranged that evil is condoned by divine softness. God is always ready to forgive but he does not take an easygoing view of sin. Nor is anything left to chance. There is a destination reserved for every created thing. It is odd that though we are reminded about this by our Lord when he talks about the very hairs on the head being numbered, the blades of grass and the lilies having their separately appointed place in God's mind, and not even a bird's death going unnoticed, we still think in terms of mass-production. Consequently we think that it cannot greatly matter to God what goes on in *my* brain, which is only one of countless million others. It matters so much that he surrounds us day and night with evidences of his will, each of them designed to recall us to the unique providence which he is exercising in our regard. On his side nothing is lacking for the perfect fulfilment of his plan. On our side all that is lacking is perfect co-operation.

The graces resulting from this will-to-will service could be numbered, subdivided, graded and pigeonholed almost indefinitely. Indeed every virtue must have God's will as its reason for existing in the first place—let alone for its perfect exercise. So rather than overcharge this aspect of the subject we can conclude with a look at the effect of surrender upon the most important of them all.

a breaking down of barriers between Jew and gentile, bond and free, Greek and Roman. All are one in Christ.

Every time we recite the Creed we acknowledge the unity and catholicity of our Faith. Charity is implied, simplicity is implied. But does the Creed lead on to logical performance? It should. Assuming that we see God's will to be working in the unity and catholicity of the Church we should not find it too difficult to rise to the next step. Unless we do—unless we base our love of neighbour upon the love and will of God—we shall be selective in our charity to others. Seeing the relationship between every human being and his neighbour, seeing also the human family in relation to God's will, we both deepen the quality and extend the scope of our charity.

Instead of driving a wedge between the twofold expressions of charity, the Christian who is himself integrated expresses charity in simplicity. He does not have to be told by a theologian that charity is undivided: he knows it. Books and sermons may be needed to tell him how to apply his charity, but his experience of God's will is all that is needed to tell him of its immanence.

The Exemplar 7

A s though to make perfectly sure that the human souls whom he had made in his own image would not miss it, God revealed his will in the form of a living person, divine and human at the same time, his Son. At the Incarnation the word of God, which is the same as the will of God, took flesh: our Lord is the will of God personified. So he is at once infinite love, truth, beauty, wisdom, perfection. He is also the way by which we go to the Father, and the life by which we live. Incorporated into his life at baptism we are members of his body and sharers of his spirit. For the guiding of our mortal affairs he is our model or exemplar. Shaping our lives according to his example and teaching, we have absolute assurance that we are fulfilling the will of God. The questions for us Christians are accordingly: how are his standards to be seen in a world which has greatly changed since his time, and how are they to be valued and applied even when they are seen?

Thinking of our Lord simply as setting the pattern of our faith, and leaving till later an examination of some of the things he said, we have even before his birth a clear enough hint as to the line to be followed in the understanding of his Father's will. Prophecy had foretold the Father's will regarding the Messias: he was to be born in Bethlehem, his mother was to be a virgin, he was to be a light to the gentiles as well as a saviour of his own people. (There were other prophecies as well, relating to his passion and death, but for the time being we shall consider only the circumstances surrounding his birth.) Notice how the providential will of God came to be fulfilled. Mary lived at Nazareth, so on the face of it there was little chance that Bethlehem would in fact be the place of Christ's birth. Mary was a virgin but since she was espoused to Joseph it might have been thought unlikely that she would become the virgin-mother of the Messias. Nevertheless God's will was moving, and unconscious agents were carrying it out. In Rome a census of the empire was decreed by Caesar Augustus. On the other side of Palestine, somewhere far to the east, scholars were drawing certain conclusions from their studies. In Bethlehem wives were becoming pregnant and giving birth. As a consequence of these apparently unrelated happenings, and in spite of what might have been expected, God's providential designs were exactly realised. Joseph, belonging to David's line, was required to register at Bethlehem, which was David's city. Mary, having consented to her vocation as delivered by Gabriel, fulfilled her role of virgin and mother. The first embassy of the gentiles, in the persons of the wise men, recognised our Lord both as

King of the Jews and the light of truth for which they had been looking. The Holy Innocents were there to cover with their martyrdom the flight into Egypt.

When people complain of the haphazard nature of their lives they should think of the apparently haphazard nature of our Lord's life, and then consider the marshalling of events, motives, and other apparently haphazard factors. It is not only in our Lord's life that everything was set for the fulfilment of the Father's will. In our own lives too everything is set and ready for our maximum co-operation. We are none of us in the lost-property office by accident. There is no such thing as, in the accepted sense, coincidence. Would you say it was coincidence that when Domitian sentenced to death those who claimed royal descent he did not include those of David's line whose poverty and obscurity ruled them out as potential pretenders, and that Joseph's insignificance as a carpenter was because his branch of the family happened to be down on its luck? Would you say it was a coincidence that somebody in Jerusalem happened to have owned a donkey which had never been used to the yoke and that a request for just such a donkey was made to him at a particular moment during the week before the Pasch? That it was a coincidence to meet a man carrying a pitcher on his head and who happened to have a room to let when these facts had been announced beforehand? That a certain rich man had happened to have a tomb ready, and not before occupied, when our Lord's body was taken down from the cross?

So the two main mistakes which people make when thinking of the providential ways of God are these. First, that the power of the Holy Spirit is brought to bear on some situations and not on others; second, that when it is brought to bear it brings an *ad hoc* decision. We should know that God's will is not only for the elect, and that when it comes down the scale to us it is just as much the expression of divine wisdom as ever it was If there were one Holy Spirit for General Councils and another for preparing a catechism class, we would have every excuse for not recognising the will of God in our own small lives: the will of God would have shrunk almost to invisibility. Fortunately for us the saints have no monopoly of the will of God. Where the saints have the advantage over us is that, being more ready to co-operate with it, they see it more often.

The second misconception is probably more common—partly because it is easier to think of the Holy Spirit acting as we would act, meeting an emergency with a snap decision, and partly because it is not at all easy to arrive at the right view of it without seeming to compromise free will. The exercise of tracing cause and effect is a hazardous one and, except in cases such as we have considered which relate to known fact, unprofitable. When we apply the process too minutely to our own past we can become victims of delusion. But allowing for all these drawbacks there is often good reason to look back and acknowledge the providential handling of what appeared at the time inexplicable or wasteful or disastrous.

Certainly there can be no danger of delusion in accepting present misfortunes, however unpromising they appear, as possible material for future good. You do not have to look only at the next life for the fruition: you can find some surprising reversals of misfortune even in this one. Job's experience was by no means unique. This is not to say that you must place all your trust in a miraculous switch; you must place all your trust in God. By trusting God to bring you through the immediate trial you dispose your soul to future graces. The immediate is seldom, if ever, the end of the affair.

If, for instance, this book which I am writing is rejected by the publisher, or if the manuscript is destroyed in a fire, I shall be disappointed. But I shall know, assuming I keep my wits about me, that out of the thought which has been put into it a new and better book may emerge. The disappointment will have been a necessary stage, part of the potential. Moreover, if there should be no end-product, and the last to be seen of the present work is a rejection slip or a little heap of ashes, nothing has been wasted. It does not mean that God never intended the book to be written in the first place, and was not helping with his will as page followed page. All it means is that one outcome has been exchanged for another, and that his will prefers this expression rather than that.

One person's blocked opportunity may liberate a hundred other people's opportunities—may even, at a different level, liberate some of his own. Our lives are so closely knit with the lives of others, and our own individual experiences are so related to one another, that to imagine we have exhausted our resources must always be wrong. The moment the potential has in fact run out will be the moment when God decides we must die. Until then we are material on the move, and our movement is having repercussions of which we have not perhaps the faintest idea. It is this thought, the thought of mutual responsibility among the members of Christ's body, which should keep people from committing suicide. The only really dead end is the taking of one's own life.

Compare an oil-painting with a piece of tapestry. If the painter is displeased with one of his figures, he can scrape the canvas and paint in another; the original composition has remained; all that has happened is that one figure went wrong and had to be taken out. With the tapestry it is a different business altogether. If the weaver is dissatisfied he cannot take out a thread, much less a figure in the group, without affecting the rest of the composition. The weaver has to go on or begin again.

So long as we live we are committed: committed to the past and the future, to other people and to God. Someone has said (and if nobody has, it is high time somebody did say) that 'what you realise after you realise it is the important thing', and if a man does not follow up his realisations—does not see them as having been made real to him by God for the express purpose of eliciting an act of his own will—he would be better off realising nothing.

The prayer *Come Holy Spirit* shows us how the will of God is meant not only to touch every point of our lives from outside but to penetrate and, in the theological sense, 'inform' every act of ours on the inside. The 'face of the earth' which has to be renewed is transformed from within. The apostle does not go about the world imposing God's will as he would pin a badge: he goes about the world so united with the will of God as to be able to kindle in others 'the fire of God's love'. He does not even go about proclaiming a law, unless it is the law of divine love which is more a matter of exchange than of rules, but rather by the help of God's grace he tries to teach men to be 'truly wise and ever rejoice in his consolations through Christ our Lord'. When he has shown them what true wisdom consists in, where to find true consolations and how to rejoice in them, he explains to them the rules they have to keep in order to express their service.

'If you love me, keep my commandments.' We will to love, but the only proof of our love is the will to obey. What love can there be without submission? So you may say that neither the will nor the love nor the law comes superimposed from without. Even the life of Christ, coming to us from the pages of the gospel, is more of an inward than an outward reality. It is born in our souls by the grace of a sacrament and developed in us by the grace of prayer and other sacraments. The Christian life does not consist in commiting to memory the historical events of the gospel and re-enacting them: the Christian life consists rather in trying to enter into the mind of Christ and living accordingly. The essential Christian purpose is to come closer to the mystery of Christ's will and model our own human will to that divine pattern.

Such then is what we mean when we speak about Christ being our model. His words are for our direction; his acts are for our inspiration and, where possible, imitation; his will is for our identification. 'I live, now not I but Christ lives in me.' Indeed unless we try to reach out from ourselves and understand something of the interior relationship between our Lord's will and the Father, between our Lord's will and human beings, between our Lord's will and the created world with all its material furnishings, it is difficult to see how we can in any true sense fulfill our Christian obligation. Without such an understanding, however elementary and (of necessity) incomplete, Christ's life means no more than a biography. It is true that his teaching provides us with a pattern of behaviour, but the experience of Christian history seems to show that a pattern of behaviour is not enough. Where Christianity has failed over the centuries is where human wills have refused to fit into the pattern, into the divine will. What is true of the Christian family at large is true of its individual members. When a man says by implication 'Christ lives, now not Christ but I live instead of him' he misses the whole point not only of Christ's life but of his own.

It comes to this then—that if the Christian refuses to let himself get involved in the life of Christ (which means in the *will* of Christ for him and for the world) he cannot expect the pattern to do the work for him. For religion to become alive, its members must contribute. The members contribute in their degree what Christ contributes in his—which is to say that they must give. They must choose. They must orientate their lives with a specific end in view. The destination as well as the direction and power of movement are given: 'I am the way and the truth and the life…no man comes to the Father but by me.'

Here we can examine the material which is provided for the twofold work proposed above, the work for the satisfactory execution of which we ask the Holy Spirit's help. The work is twofold because we look beyond our own personal sanctification ('send forth thy Spirit and our hearts shall be created') to the evangelisation and sanctification of mankind ('and thou shalt renew the face of the earth'). We have as means for the undertaking the Creed and the life and teaching of our Lord. The Church supplies aid with both certainty of interpretation and the graces of the sacraments. How, it might be thought by a visitor from another planet, can we possibly go wrong? Ideally speaking, there should be no discrepancy between man's Christian beliefs and his engagement in everyday life. But committed to a material world, and spinning out his mortality in time sequences, he is always more or less conscious of his failure here: he deviates from the course laid down.

'Faith,' says Danielou, 'offers a vision of the world which embraces all things in the perspective of God's plan. God is at work in our midst; we are impelled to be his co-workers.' Yes, but even with this vision and with this impulse we are at best unprofitable workers. And sometimes hardly co-workers at all. Why do we limp in this service, the service which we know to be worth while and which cannot, of its very nature, ask more of us than we can bear to give? Surely it is because we have, again, never fully made our own the implications of the mystery of the Incarnation. If to us Christ was *really* the exemplar, really as compelling as he was, say to Zachaeus or Mary Magdalen or Paul, would we not accept faith's offer of 'a vision of the world which embraces all things in the perspective of God's plan' and apply, day in and day out for the whole of our lives, the lessons of that vision?

Back then to the wisdom of Bethlehem, Nazareth, Galilee, and Calvary. How does our surrender match its summons? First there are the circumstances surrounding the nativity: lack of comfort, signs of not being wanted by those who might have been expected to help, no guarantee that on the material side matters would improve, loneliness at being in a strange place, uncertainty about the return home. These are things which everyone has experienced at one time or another, but the fact that they were experienced by the most important family in the history of man should draw our attention to the will which arranges them. We should be grateful for being in the authentic tradition. If we want to know what God thinks we are worth we might do worse than reflect upon what he sends us. We know how the Holy Family stands in the Father's sight, and if we can find any share at all in the neglect which they were allowed to suffer at the hands of their fellow human beings we have reason to congratulate ourselves.

Moving from the infancy to the ministry, we find the same summons to faith. The natural is accounted for in the dimension of the supernatural. The riddle of human existence can be solved only by the divine wisdom who posed it, and when wisdom itself assumes human life and explains how we are to proceed the way is clear. But clear only to those who accept his terms. His terms are himself. His terms are the Father's will to which he, the Son, was obedient 'even unto death'. Without faith in the validity of our Lord's claims—among them being the claim that he was the perfect fulfilment of the Father's will —a man is forced back upon the historical and the rational. Such a man can see that every now and again in our Lord's life there was reasonable expectation of success: when discovered as a boy in the Temple he showed promise of great things; on the shores of Tiberias there was a move to make him king; it was freely admitted that he spoke more convincingly than any of the leaders of his time; on Palm Sunday there was a popular demonstration and he entered the capital in triumph. But from here onwards the way is by no means clear to the man without faith. If the historical is strained to the utmost in the story of the resurrection, the rational fails completely.

Take the passion itself, ending with the death which to reason means defeat and to faith the climax. Again the lesson is that if we want to know the connection between God's will and suffering we have only to look at who it was who took on the whole of God's will and who suffered more than anyone else in all history. Getting near to the mystery of the Son's passion is like getting near to the mystery of the Father's will: there has to be the act of surrender. One single hour of suffering, taken as the will of God, does more for the soul than any amount of sensible devotion.

The demand of faith which the passion makes of us is something more than the mere notional consent which we give to the facts as revealed in the gospels: the challenge is to our experience. In our own sufferings, such as they are, God's grace is inviting us to active participation with those of our Lord. One of the main obstacles to our doing this—to the voluntary act of uniting our trials with his—is that we cannot imagine how our pinprick pains can be of any use to him. Nor can we imagine how the Second Person of the Blessed Trinity can be subject to the same sort of things that bother us. Until we have convinced ourselves of the truth that our Lord could feel depressed, could feel the force of temptation, could be disappointed in people whom he loved, we have missed one of the most significant lessons which Christ came to teach. So as to win our experimental knowledge of his passion he puts his own experience at our disposal, and so that we should have more to learn of his passion we put our experience at his. Understood rightly, and not merely accepted as a doctrine, the passion takes us to the very edge of human experience. Not all of us are called to follow as far as 'If this chalice may not pass away but I must drink it, thy will be done, and perhaps very few indeed to the point of 'My God, my God, why hast thou forsaken me,' but the experience of Christ is there —for the sharing.

Always in the last analysis it is the mystery of faith. The Blessed Sacrament is called exactly that: *mysterium fidei*. The passion, the ordering of the universe, human free will and the foreknowledge of God, grace moving infallibly within an organisation composed of ordinary human beings: *mysteria fidei*. Life, with its unending conflict between reason and faith, can find security only in acceptance. Those who think that reason has the last word go one way; those who cling to faith go another. Goodness knows what goes on in the mind of the rationalist, but are we to believe that in the mind of the man who·chooses to walk by faith the rationalist conclusion no longer presses? Of course it does. The difference lies in the choice, the firmness of the choice, and the fidelity with which the will abides by the choice. 'We must have great faith,' says Mouroux in his book *The Meaning of Man*, 'if we are to arrive at the harmonious union of the world.' Yes indeed, and we must also have great faith if we are to arrive at a harmonious union within ourselves.

A Spanish philosopher, Miguel de Unamuno, wrote a number of novels which had as their theme the struggle of human existence. Man, never quite sure of his convictions, drives himself desperate with his search for truth. But what qualifies is neither the uncertainty nor the desperation but the unremitting quest for truth. More fancifully, it is suggested that just as the writer of fiction relies on his characters to put across his message, so God needs human beings as a medium for his revelation. More fancifully still, Unamuno suggests that if the novelist can dream up people out of his own head and give them being, may not God be doing the same—may not we be simply God's dream? May not the whole of human existence be no more than what God happens to be dreaming? Theologians would probably have something to say about his idea (which makes the elemental instinct for survival express itself in man's most imperative prayer, 'Dream us, O Lord') but if you substitute 'willing' for 'dreaming' you need not be so far out. If the concept is disagreeable which makes us issue from a divine reverie there is nothing disagreeable about being deliberately created by the all-wise will of God. Correspondingly, it is not for a deity to issue from the dreams of man, and this is what in effect takes place when a man defines his own private religion. Subjective religion, selecting and interpreting and changing back and forth, dreams up not only its own standards but also the nature of its own source.

Back then to the surrender of the human will and reason to divine will and reason. How to do it, where to find our practical, viable plan? Christ the perfect exemplar, God and man, the divine will made actual, divine love made imitable.

Summing Up 8

IF WHAT our Lord did and suffered brings us nearer to doing and suffering in the name of the Father's will, what he preached and prayed should do the same. He had been foretold as 'the man of sorrows and acquainted with
The prophecy related to his interior life. But there were other prophecies which related to his exterior life, to his work and message. He was hailed by Isaias as 'prince of peace,' and seven centuries later by Zachary, the father of John the Baptist, as 'the Orient from on high' who would visit the world 'to enlighten them that sit in darkness and in the shadow of death, to direct our feet into the way of peace.' So it is of first importance that we should know something about this peace which he was to establish and this light which he was to spread.

In our Lord's mission on earth, two elements stand out as surpassing all others: the work of redeeming mankind, and the work of founding his Church. This *was* the peace which he had come to bring, this *was* the light which he had come to spread. It might be said that every recorded act of his, and every recorded sermon, bore upon one or other of these elements. Now he has told us that we must learn of him, that we must come to the Father by way of him, that his is the peace which he alone can give and which the world cannot disturb, that his is the light without which man works in darkness. He is the shepherd, the vine, the word, the name by which miracles are worked and prayers heard.

Such richness of illustration and identification overwhelms us, and we start casting about for a formula which will express all our Lord's activities in one. Fortunately there is no lack of texts which give us what we want. Our formula, differently phrased in different passages of the New Testament, contains the essential quality which we have been considering throughout this book. 'My meat is to do the will of him that sent me,' our Lord says at the well in Samaria, 'that I may perfect his work.' 'I seek not my own will,' he says when he is attacked for making himself equal to the Father, 'but the will of him that sent me.' He repeats this phrase almost word for word when asked for a sign, when asked for 'true bread from heaven'. Our Lord was perfectly fulfilling the Messianic psalm which makes him say, 'Behold, I come to do thy will, O God'. The point which we are trying to make here is simply that it was *by* doing the Father's will that Christ redeemed mankind and founded a Church. So that right at the end of his life he was able to say, 'it is finished: I have done the work which thou gavest me to do.' The Father had willed the redemption of man and the foundation of the Church. Inseparably united with the will of his Father, Christ knew that nothing of the Father's will was left to be done on earth: he could now continue the union in heaven.

So much for the relationship between our Lord's outward accomplishment and inward union. What has he to say about ours? The story is parallel and again the texts are abundant. 'Not everyone who says to me, "Lord, Lord," shall enter into the kingdom of heaven,' Christ explains when pointing out that a tree is judged by its fruits, 'but he who does the will of my Father who is in heaven.' The response has to be that of obedience, not that of emotion or habit or professional pride. The same demand for a deliberate choice, when superficial impulse may incline the other way, is stressed in the parable of the two sons which ends with the question which a child of five would be able to answer: 'which of the two' —one of whom was all eagerness to work but did not, the other reluctant but finally obedient— 'did the father's will?' Again there is that vivid scene given by St. Mark which shows our Lord so pressed with his work of preaching that Mary and some of his relations have to send messages to say they would like to speak to him: 'Who is my mother and my brethren?...whosoever shall do the will of God, he is my brother and my sister and my mother.' Lastly, when he tells us how to pray he insists that our disposition should be that of readiness to do God's will. Without 'thy will be done' there would seem to be little point in praying at all. With it, there is nothing that may not be prayed for, and no reason why the prayer should ever stop.

We could go through the epistles, combing them for references to the necessity for surrender to the Father's will. 'He who does the will of God,' says St. John, 'abides for ever.' 'That doing the will of God,' we read in Hebrews, 'you may receive the promise.' St. Paul to the Romans: 'Be not conformed to this world, but be reformed in the newness of your mind, that you may prove what is the good and the acceptable and the perfect will of God.' 'Not serving the eye,' St. Paul warns the Ephesians, 'but as servants of Christ doing the will of God from the heart.' He tells the Colossians how Epaphras is constantly praying for them that they 'may stand perfect and full in all the will of God.' There is testimony everywhere you look: the early Church was fed on the will of God, the word of God, the law of God.

We accept all this, and indeed there is no getting away from it if we have any faith at all, but the difficulty for most of us is keeping it up. Both keeping up the appreciation of the doctrine and the will to put the doctrine into effect. Our Lord saw this weakness in us when he said, 'If you *continue* in my word, then shall you be my disciples indeed; and you shall know the truth and the truth shall make you free.' The idea of service carries with it the idea of perseverance. The connotation is not so immediate today as it used to be, because room-service and car-service and similar passing acts of service have brought along a new element, but certainly when we talk about the service of God we do not think of something intermittent. If God's will is a constant living actuality, our response should follow suit.

Too many people imagine that in order to serve God generously they must be living lives which they do not like. This is a misconception which deters people from embarking upon such a service because they do not see themselves persevering indefinitely. These are the people who understand about the first half of the text just quoted but who have missed the point about the second. The reward of continuing in God's service is knowledge of the truth—the truth 'which makes you free,' not 'which makes you miserable'. Enjoying the liberty of the children of God, the soul enjoys life. There is a great difference between a life of self-sacrifice which is the Christian ideal and the life of self-torture with which we often identify the Christian ideal.

God gives us our lives to lead, and it is ungracious of us if we hate every minute of those lives. As we have seen, God's will may (and on occasion must) involve suffering, loneliness, boredom; but suffering, loneliness, boredom are not designed to make up the whole of life. We are not meant to be in the flame from morning till night, and certainly we are not meant to congratulate ourselves if we are. We are told to 'rejoice in the Lord... everywhere give thanks...make of our sacrifice a pleasing offering,' which clearly we cannot do if we cannot associate God's will with peace and liberty but only with conflict and darkness. If it is true that 'God's providence is my inheritance' then I have inherited peace. I cannot proclaim my trust in providence and at the same time deny my peace. It may not be the bland tranquility of rest which follows my surrender to the providence of God, but then I have not bargained for the smooth. It will be the tranquility of order, it will be beyond the reach of foreboding, and will rely upon foundations more sure than any I could lay by careful planning. And as such is something to be thankful for.

Which brings us to the question of gratitude. We have seen how God's will is inseparable from himself. Consequently it is true to say that we are receiving expressions of himself, evidences of himself, little private revelations of himself if you like, at every turn. If this is so, ought we not to be giving thanks—if not all the time at least as often as we can? In a superior sort of way, perhaps, we smile a superior sort of smile when nuns say *Deo gratias* every few minutes and at the slightest thing. But they are right to say it. Let it be hoped they mean it. The slightest thing deserves gratitude. Without thinking, we rely upon God's providence from moment to moment, so to make a habit of thinking about it and giving thanks is bound to bring us closer to God. We depend upon God for the air we breathe, but who gives thanks for air? The habit of conforming to God's will and the habit of thanking for it go together. That is why we find the saints brimming over with gratitude about everything: they live in perpetual acknowledgement.

Consider the difference which this must make to the life of prayer. Recollection becomes the more or less normal thing. Where before it was the pleasureable which elicited acts of gratitude, now it is the conformity which produces them. The question at this stage is not whether the particular circumstance is pleasurable or painful, but whether the will can rise to it and be grateful for it. Accordingly, with conformity to the providential plan as its foundation, prayer becomes not so much a series of acts as a state. The condition on which it operates is solely the will of God, and the will of God is in constant operation.

Whether such prayer is seen as receptive or co-operative, as contemplative or discursive, it makes for the habit of gratitude. The thankful realisation that all things come from God becomes second nature and the reason for living. The air we breathe may be cold or foggy or damp, but what difference does that make? We cannot go on breathing without it.

In the section above we have talked about perseverance, peace, gratitude, and prayer. In

113

case the connection between these is not at once obvious we will emphasize the truth that there exists in fact a very considerable link. You have only to put the qualities in reverse to see how instability, insecurity, ingratitude, and neglect of prayer must destroy the exchange between the soul and God. Not until final perseverance is rewarded, peace eternally established, gratitude assumed into everlasting prayer before God's throne, shall we fully appreciate the synthesis. But in the meantime, while engaged on this journey which paradoxically finds its term only in infinity, we can proceed in unity. What has been described as 'the happening of the saints to their vision' can be anticipated even by us who are beginners.

Hitherto we have dwelt upon aspects of peace and unity with regard to the soul. In the remaining pages we can investigate peace and unity in their wider context. More important than our own selves is the human race, and questions which have to do with world order are not as academic and remote as they may seem when we read about them in the papers. We should know that because God's will is working in the world as well as in us the condition of the world is our concern. No part of God's will is excluded from our interest, and the part which relates to the spread of Christ's peace is every Christian's responsibility.

From the first Christmas day, when the *Gloria in excelsis Deo* announced peace to men of good-will, until April 11, 1963, when Pope John XXIII issued his encyclical letter *Pacem in terris* to the world, the message has been the same. And in the year of this writing, John's successor, Pope Paul VI, is working on his predecessor's legacy. The present-day version of the Christmas hymn is roughly this: peace results from the order implanted by God in the heart of man; it means peace with God, peace with fellow men, peace with authority. Such is the main theme of *Pacem in terris*. Commentators in the press, non-Catholic as well as Catholic, seem agreed that the encyclical is one of the most moving documents of recent years. Moving to what? Not, if we are to judge by what has since happened in the world, to action.

The words of a holy religious leader may move the heart to tears, may even move the intellect to conviction, but unless they also move the will to take action the situation remains where it was. This is where the individual can play his part, even if it remains a very small one. According to Pope John, peace radiates from the individual. 'The world will never be the dwelling-place of peace,' he says, 'until peace has found a home in each and every man, until every man preserves within himself the order ordained by God to be preserved.' Peace, like liberty and truth and the will of God itself, is not static but dynamic.

We, who by God's grace have 'looked into the perfect law of liberty' and found peace in Christ, owe an obligation towards the spread of truth and order. We may not sit still and imagine we have satisfied our responsibilities by offering some of our prayers at Mass for the intentions of the Holy Father. The world is moving, and the Church with it: 'they must upward still and onward, who would keep abreast of Truth.' Granted that the starting-off place is the human soul, there has to be a start. And how, when you really get down to it, is a start to be made—and in what direction?

First we have to make ourselves familiar with the nature of what the gospel is now being called upon to face. This need not involve an intensive course of study: it calls for conditioning our minds to the fact that there is an emergency in the world and that we may not evade it. Whether we like it or not we are caught up in it. We can either allow ourselves to be caught up as leaves in a spiral of wind or we can join the whirl and try to show that it is spinning round by the will of God and that Christ is at its centre. It will be a question of orientation: am I thinking of other people's needs in regard to God or am I thinking only of my own? Is the peace which God has designed for mankind receiving any sort of contribution from me, or do I think of peace as a personal commodity which is best safeguarded by my refusal to get mixed up with outside affairs? Surely what was meant by Pope John's *aggiornamento* was precisely this: the recognition that the will of God could be moving in a fast-changing society and that tradition must keep up with it. The implication is not that tradition must be sacrificed; on the contrary the implication is that it should be made more use of—in the contemporary setting.

A man whose world is limited to his family and friends and the people whom he meets at his work might well object at this point that his horizons are too restricted for participation in world affairs. 'If God had wanted me to extend the life of Christ in the contemporary setting he would have placed me in a better position to do so. Either I would have been called to be a public relations officer or I would have been allowed the time and the talent to study the question. As things are, I have as much as I can do to fulfill the obligations I learned as a child from the catechism. I am too set in my ways to start modernising and updating my religion to suit the changing scene.' The objection would be valid if the demand were for a headlong plunge into the ecclesiastical arena. But nobody is asking you to plunge into the ecclesiastical arena—unless of course you happen to be an ecclesiastic, in which case you are expected to make a highly professional performance in the environment where God has placed you—but only to attend to what is going on in your own arena and, if necessary, to widen its boundaries. Nobody is asking you to concern yourself with public relations but it may well be God's will that you should give more attention to perfecting your private relations. What is demanded is a more planned and, given the right circumstances, a more extended, application of traditional Christianity.

Much in this will depend upon the God-given sphere of influence. To the foreign secretary of a sovereign nation the opportunity of furthering Christian ideals would be considerable; to someone who is bedridden it would be less so. But, as we shall see before leaving the subject, there is no time in a person's life when the effort to impart the peace, truth, and life of Christ may be laid aside. Pope John was careful to include the laity in the apostolic mission, urging men and women to see their secular callings in a supernatural light and to direct their professional enterprise towards specifically Christian ends. *Pacem in terris* presents the Church as a unity, and not as divided between the official and the unofficial. If in the past there has been a gap between those responsible for the management and mechanism of the Church and those responsible for accepting what they get, such a gap must be bridged. The members of the Church are members of its mission: this was understood in the early Church and is coming to be better understood today. But there was a long period when it was not understood and, despite successive pontificates in our own time which have pointed to the original concept, there is always the danger of making artificial divisions in at least three of the Church's four essential marks.

Following the first recommendation—that we should convince ourselves of need and opportunity —must come the exhortation to do something about it. Relating how we behave to what we believe has never been our strong point as Christians. It might be said that it has never been anybody's strong point, whether Christian or not. True, but the member of Christ's Church has more support: laws, sacraments, doctrines—everything is laid down for him and he gets the grace to pick it up and act on it. How then cope with this dichotomy (keenly felt by St. Paul as he tells his friends in Rome, 'I see another law in my members warring against the law in my mind') so that we come to be ruled by what we believe rather than what our fallen natures prompt us to? St. Paul gives the answer when he says that the only force strong enough to resolve the difficulty is 'the grace of God by Christ our Lord'. When the human will has chosen the Father's will and is living it in the life of the Son, there is order in the soul and neither weakness nor passion has the final say.

It is this order which somehow or other has to be communicated to a disordered world. Having become ordered ourselves—our senses and emotions subject to reason and will, our reason and will subject to God—we have something to offer to a society in conflict. By operating as a whole human being, the mature person that God intends me to be, I can unite with other whole and mature human beings and work towards the wholeness and maturity of mankind. Here is the synthesis of Christian faith and Christian action which results in peace, the peace envisaged by the *Gloria in excelsis* and *Pacem in terris* alike.

Very well then—you are not a foreign minister, not a member of the administration, not a union leader, not a political broadcaster or a columnist. Measure it down to size, and make a realistic judgment of your powers as seen against the background of the life to which God has called you. Are you going to tell me that you see no warring elements in the environment which meets you in your work, in your home, in your social contacts? And, having admitted that such warring elements exist, are you going to tell me that you are utterly powerless in the cause of harmony? We are not talking now of how to effect the restoration of order—each case is unique and must call for the exercise of the practical judgment—but of why we must want to. Like us, other people are members of Christ's body. There must be order in Christ's body: the members must be subject to the head and at one with each other. Otherwise the body is divided, which is what the world is today.

Without stepping out of his environment, every man must reduce division and promote order. Take someone in the teaching profession who is concerned about preserving Christian principles in a system of education which leaves them out of account. Is he to look the other way? Is he, without a protest, to choose some other career in which this conflict will not come up? Or someone in the medical profession who sees operations performed which are at variance with his Catholic conscience. Or a lawyer who sees injustice in much that he is supposed to be standing for. Or a religious who finds that the order or congregation to which he belongs is departing from its essential spirit. Or a boy or girl in school who believes the atmosphere of the place to constitute a threat to faith or morals. Are not all these people pledged to pursue the Christian ideal? In every environment there must be struggle and contradiction, and it is everyone's duty to make a bid for order. Christ's order is not always man's ('my peace I give unto you, not as the world gives') but it is always for Christ's followers to point to it. In an age when questions of marriage, race relations, total war, strikes, sex education, capital punishment and compulsory state controls are live issues it is important that we set our standards by the mind of Christ.

It might be thought that far from spreading harmony, such tactics as we talk about would be more likely to cause further friction. Here again is where *Pacem in terris* has an answer. 'Peace is but an empty word if it does not rest upon (the) order that is founded upon truth, built on justice, nourished and animated by charity, and brought into effect under the auspices of freedom.' Truth, justice, charity: these are as much Pope John's theme as they are the theme of the prophet Isaias. Our encounter with others, whether they are co-religionists or not, is in charity and not in battle. A happier term than 'encounter' is the now more popular one, 'exchange', suggesting a mutual opening up. Indeed the whole ecumenical movement is conditioned by the readiness to explore, in the interests of peace and justice and truth, the minds of other people and to let other people explore ours. If charity is not the channel of this exchange, the exchange will not take place. Truth and justice will suffer.

'Human society as we here picture it,' says Pope John again, 'demands that men be guided by justice, that they respect the rights of others and do their duty.' This is where freedom comes in to its own, because though there can be no true freedom where truth is not accepted, neither can there be true freedom where there is religious intolerance. Charity must underlie our every attempt to evangelise or our apostolate is no more than propaganda. 'It (human society) demands too that they be animated by such love,' the encyclical goes on, 'as will make them feel the needs of others as their own, and induce them to share their goods with others, and to strive in the world to make all men alike heirs to the noblest of intellectual and spiritual values.' The range of charity is as boundless here as it is in the Sermon on the Mount. The barricades are down, and liberty is now given a clear run. 'For human society thrives on freedom, namely on the use of means which are consistent with the dignity of its individual members, who, being endowed with reason, assume responsibility for their own actions.' St. Paul puts the case for the freedom which is born of charity when he says, 'You are not under the law but under grace...love is the fulfilment of the law.'

Sin, by destroying charity, repudiates order and makes freedom impossible. Life in Christ is lost and fallen man reverts to his fallen state. All this may seem doctrinaire and remote but when we apply it to the will of God it has particular relevance. What it amounts to is that sin shuts out the will of God, hinders its action in the world, imprisons man within himself and lays such a crust of selfishness over his soul that the working of grace cannot be properly seen. The man who has chosen sin has chosen to accept as part of life the anomalies and contradictions which find no place in God's antecedent will: social injustice, scientific nihilism, immorality—these things are no longer negations to him. Love has so far died in him that the flaws and scars are assumed to be of little or no importance.

Lastly but more briefly (since this is what the whole of this book has been about and repetition wearies) there is the contribution to the world's need which the individual soul can make in the way of prayer and penance. When we pray we accept and praise God's will; when we accept our sufferings voluntarily we praise God's will. For the evils of the world there is no therapy like that of prayer and penance. We have this on the authority of our Lord himself when he was talking to his disciples about exorcism. The beauty of it is that while there may be doubt as to how we are to fulfill our obligation as apostles of peace and love, there is no such difficulty when it comes to the practice of prayer and penance. Knowing that such an apostolate is bound to benefit mankind, all we have to do is to get on with it. As our prayer deepens and as our resignation under trial becomes more purified, the scope of our apostolate will become more clear. It will be seen as something all-embracing because it will come from the heart which has Christ at its centre. 'We used to say that the mission field was on the map,' wrote an American Methodist, Stanley Jones, 'but now I know it is in the heart.' Pope John would have agreed with him. This is truly ecumenical, truly the spirit of *aggiornamento*, truly a reconciliation.

After offering the bread and wine at Mass, the priest prays 'for our salvation and that of the whole world'. In the Christian concept prayer is dynamic, and the salvation worked for is universal.

Looked at in its essential terms of fulfilling the will of God, religion should grow from being a part-time commitment to being a whole-time attitude of mind. The actual exercises of religion may be various, and the temperature in which they are carried out may fluctuate, but when the human will has identified itself with him who wills all, then a man may confidently say, 'I will now not I but God wills in me.'

Qui pro vobis et pro multis tradetur in remissione peccatorum. The blood of Christ does not stand still. Nor is it shed for the few. The Incarnation and Redemption were for all, and their work is still going on.